1979

CHAUCER
Lyric and Allegory

GEOFFREY CHAUCER

CHAUCER

LYRIC AND ALLEGORY

Edited with an Introduction,
Notes and Glossary
by

JAMES REEVES

BARNES & NOBLE, Inc.
NEW YORK
PUBLISHERS & BOOKSELLERS SINCE 1873

GEOFFREY CHAUCER 1343?–1400

INTRODUCTION, NOTES AND GLOSSARY
© JAMES REEVES 1970

FIRST PUBLISHED IN THE UNITED STATES 1971,
BY BARNES & NOBLE, INC.

ISBN 389 04071 1

TO

MICHAEL IRWIN

Printed in Great Britain

CONTENTS

PREFACE

WHAT is the justification for making a selection from Chaucer's poems which excludes all of the *Canterbury Tales*? First, there are many useful editions of the *Tales*, either singly or in groups, and most readers who are likely to come across the present selection will already be familiar with some at least of the *Tales*, or at any rate with the General Prologue. Secondly, editions of the other poems, with the exception of *Troilus and Criseyde*, are comparatively rare; accordingly they are little known, except by the specialist. Yet even he may not want to read all the other poems in their entirety. There are long dull passages in many of them – passages where Chaucer seems to have become bored with the task he had set himself, or which had been set him by a patron. Accordingly, selection is desirable because among these poems are many which are worthy of more attention than they have received. Indeed, the wholly admirable attention which has been given to the *Tales* from Skeat's pioneering work onwards has had the effect that Chaucer's other poems have been unduly neglected by the non-specialist reader. But the very concentration on the *Tales* has so familiarised the educated reader with the language of Chaucer that he is now in a better position than ever to read and appreciate the other poems. These poems will offer to many readers a new range of poetic experience. There are many passages which the enthusiast for Chaucer will want to make his own, as surely as he has made the *Pardoner's Tale*, the *Nun's Priest's Tale* or the *Wife of Bath's Prologue*.

This selection aims, too, at making a contribution to Chaucer studies: one which can be summed up by asking, How good, how important a poet would Chaucer seem to us if he had never written the *Tales*? In the Introduction I have given a sketch of Chaucer's life and his position in relation to contemporary society. I have outlined his contribution to the evolution of poetry, and have put forward some ideas about the most fruitful ways in which to appreciate the poems. Above all, however, I have subordinated historical considerations to the consideration of how best to enjoy these unfamiliar poems for their own sake. Like most pre-Tudor poets, Chaucer has been for too long the almost exclusive study of students and scholars often more interested in philology than in poetry. The principal justification of this selection, then, is that it is poetry in its own right, transferred from the specialist's desk to the hands of the poetically educated common reader.

I have been greatly helped, throughout my work on this book, by Duncan Beal, Stephen Coote and Martin Ryle, whose indispensable services I wish to acknowledge with sincere gratitude. For valuable suggestions in making my selection, and especially in revising the Introduction, I am greatly indebted to Michael Irwin of the University of Kent. For the final form of the latter, and for whatever shortcomings it retains, I am, however, solely responsible.

I wish also to record my indebtedness to the authors of the critical and editorial works listed in the bibliography, particularly the splendid and exhaustive edition of Professor F. N. Robinson. For permission to reproduce the Harvard Portrait, which appears as a frontispiece, I have to thank the Houghton Library of Harvard University.

J. R.

INTRODUCTION

I

GEOFFREY CHAUCER, believed to have been born about 1343, was the son of John and Agnes Chaucer of Ipswich. John Chaucer, probably of French descent (the name in its French form is Chaussier, *shoemaker*), was a prosperous wine merchant with Court connections. The young Geoffrey served as a page in the household of Lionel, Duke of Clarence, where he probably met John of Gaunt, the patron through whom he won the favour of the Lancastrians which supported him all his life. He is next heard of in the English army in France. Taken prisoner near Rheims, his ransom was paid in part by King Edward III. By 1367 he was in the royal service and travelled to the Continent on frequent diplomatic missions. About this time he married Philippa Roet, who was in the service of Queen Philippa. Her sister, Katherine Swynford, became the wife of John of Gaunt. Philippa Chaucer died in 1387. Chaucer continued to enjoy the royal favour and to receive a series of commercial and diplomatic appointments. At this time no serious gap existed between commercial and diplomatic missions. Such missions were of prime importance in the development of Chaucer's mind and writing. His earlier travels brought him into contact with French authors, and at about the age of twenty-nine he was in Italy, where he made his first acquaintance with Italian literature. He visited Genoa and Florence, and may have met Petrarch and perhaps Boccaccio. These two poets, together with Dante, were crucially influential on the growth of Chaucer's work.

In 1374 he was appointed Controller of the Customs in the Port of London and was granted, rent-free, the use of a house above Aldgate. During the 1370's he received further marks of the royal favour and became increasingly prosperous. However, in 1377 Edward III was succeeded by Richard II, then in his minority, and Chaucer seems to have incurred the displeasure of the regent, Gloucester. But when Richard came to his majority, the favour of the Lancastrians was once more in evidence. In 1385 Chaucer became a Justice of the Peace in the county of Kent, where he went to live on losing his house in London. The following year he became Knight of the Shire but sat in Parliament for one session only.

In 1389, when Richard II came of age, Chaucer began a two years' appointment as Clerk of the King's Works, with responsibility for the maintenance of such important buildings as the Tower of London and the Palace of Westminster. In the course of the frequent journeys which this work entailed Chaucer was robbed more than once, on one occasion with violence. His retirement from this post in 1390 gave him more time for poetry, though the precise reason for his giving up the Clerkship is not known. The following year he was appointed Deputy Forester of the Royal Forest of North Petherton in Somerset, but what exactly this involved is not clear. This last official appointment may have been little more than a sinecure intended to reward him for his many and various services to the Crown.

Chaucer's movements during the last ten years of his life are not known. All that is certain is that Richard continued to use him favourably. On the accession of Henry IV in 1399 Chaucer suffered, like other adherents of the King, from some anxiety lest the royal favour should be withdrawn. However, the new King confirmed the various royal grants, and there is probably little truth in the notion that Chaucer's last years were spent in poverty. He died on 25 October 1400, if the words on his tomb in Westminster Abbey are to be believed.

This bare and partly negative chronicle gives most of the significant facts which are known with reasonable certainty. Every aspect of Chaucer's life and personality, his Court and family connections, has been the subject of exhaustive study; it is not unfair to say that much of this scholarship has been occupied with refuting the theories of other scholars. What was his education? When exactly was he married, and did he have a second wife? Who were his children? The answers to these questions are not known. Nor is it known from any evidence outside his own writings what were his own interests and personal habits. When it is added that the 'little Lewis' for whom Chaucer wrote his *Treatise on the Astrolabe* is thought to have been his son, that is all that can reasonably be assumed about his family life. It seems reasonable also to assume that he was at any rate partially educated in one of the Inns of Court, since that would be the likely education of a man of his position. This supposition rests on a tradition, once discredited but now rehabilitated, that he was fined two shillings as a Templar for beating a Franciscan friar in Fleet Street. Flimsy as is the evidence for this tradition, it is the only thing believed about Chaucer which has any semblance of a personal anecdote. The public records of Chaucer's career make no mention whatever of his work as a poet. He must, however, have enjoyed the friendship of the principal writers of his time. The poet John Gower was certainly a friend. He also probably knew the contemporary French poets, Deschamps and Machaut, both influential in the development of his early style.

Chaucer's major English and Scottish contemporaries and successors were unanimous in their tributes to his genius.

> And eke my master Chauceris nowe is grave
> The noble rethor Poete of breteine
> That worthy was the laurer to have
> Of poetrie and the palme atteine
> That made firste to distille and reyne
> The golde dewe droppis of speche and eloquence
> In-to oure tounge thourgh his excellence
> And founde the flourys first of rethoryk
> Oure rude speche oonly to enlumyne
> That in oure tunge was never noon him like.

This is John Lydgate, writing a decade after Chaucer's death. Thomas Hoccleve, about the same time, also refers to Chaucer's importance in the field of linguistic innovation, calling him

The firste fyndere of our faire langage.

Later in the fifteenth century writers began to praise Chaucer for the graphic pithiness that has been admired ever since. The anonymous author of *The Book of Curtesye* (1477) says:

> Redith his werkis ful of plesaunce
> Clere in sentence in langauge excellent
> Briefly to wryte suche was his suffysance
> Whatever to seye he toke in his entente
> His langage was so fayr and pertynente
> It semeth unto mannys heerynge
> Not only the worde but verely the thynge.

Chaucer's first printer, William Caxton, writing about 1480, says of the poet that

he comprehended hys maters in short quyck and hye sentences eschewyng prolyxyte castyng away the chaf of superfluyte and shewyng the pyked [picked] grayn of sentence uttered by crafty and sugred eloquence.

It seems also, to judge from Skelton's *Phillip Sparrow*, written a century after Chaucer's death, that some readers had already decided that his 'obscurities' required emendation. Skelton, the poet, however, writing of Chaucer's English, is forthright in acclaiming his absolute clarity of expression:

> And now men wold have amended
> His english, where at they barke,
> And marre all they warke:
> Chaucer, that famous Clarke,
> His tearmes were not darcke,
> But pleasaunt, easy, and playne;
> No worde he wrote in vayne.

In an unusually turbulent period of English history, he did not, as did some contemporary writers, inveigh openly against the evils of his time; it is safe to assume that, depending as he did on Lancastrian patronage, he preferred to keep out of public controversy. We can, of course, infer from his poems what his attitude was, for instance, to corruption in the Church. He is said to have known Wycliffe. But he did not directly and explicitly attack the evils of the Church, as did the author of *Piers Plowman*.

Chaucer's poetry mirrors, but does not on the whole criticise, the society in which he lived. He was interested more in knowing than in improving men and women. He was concerned with the permanent features of the human comedy, not the distortions wrought on human nature by the shortcomings of social organisation. A good deal has been written about the social life of the second half of the fourteenth century in England – its ecclesiastical troubles, its dynastic and military feuds, the evil consequences of the Black Death, the Peasants' Revolt, the growing strength and influence of the trading classes. But all these things make their appearance only on the fringe of Chaucer's poetry: they are referred to in passing. There are numerous topical references to events of the day, but they remain marginal. We know, in short, much of the world in which Chaucer moved as a favoured state official; we know that he was an intimate member of a gifted Court circle. But what he thought of the world of the Court and the world that revolved about it we can only infer from his poems.

II

The man who emerges from the foregoing account is no more than a distinguished civil servant with literary leanings. It would suffice as the life of perhaps dozens of others of his time who do not happen to be identified as the author of *The Canterbury Tales*. Yet when we come to look for internal evidence as to the nature and personality of this author, the result is hardly less vague and suppositious. Chaucer was, essentially, a dramatic poet. (I shall refer later to the more subjective, 'confessional' element in his writings.) Like Shakespeare, he was concerned with men and women, their passions and opinions, the thoughts and ideas which made them act as they did. Commentators have argued themselves to a standstill to prove that this or that speech in one of the plays represents Shakespeare's 'view' of monarchy, religion or politics. There is no evidence that Shakespeare's conception of society corresponds, as has been asserted, with Ulysses' speech on Degree in *Troilus and Cressida*, rather than with the attitude of Hector, Thersites or Achilles. It is truer to say that, being a poet, not a theologian or a social scientist, he was interested, even to the point of multiple self-identification for the time being, with *all* views on all matters. As a dramatist, he was concerned with the interactions of these views.

Chaucer too was a poet, first and foremost. He was a dramatic poet in the sense that he was concerned with men and women and with poetic form as the medium of expression for that concern. His outlook on society was not didactic or theoretical, it was exploratory, analytical. His outlook on literature was not simply adaptive or absorptive, it was critical. It follows that it is difficult, if not impossible, to take his poems, as we say, 'at their face value'. Whenever we are tempted to do so, the thought comes to us that he was perhaps, in this instance, parodying the manner in which he was writing. Many of the poems in this selection are among those of Chaucer's apprenticeship, and the mark of this apprenticeship is a continuous critical awareness of the merits and demerits of the material at hand in the work of other poets. His implied criticism of poets and poetry, while usually genial in its satiric tone, is nonetheless keen. He wrote for an audience, a Court audience, and was usually shrewd and cautious in expressing his attitude to the kind of poetry the Court enjoyed. He wore, therefore, a mask of irony. It is never easy to penetrate an ironist's mask. Take, for instance, his references to himself – as conspicuous in his poetry as they are lacking in Shakespeare's. Consider the picture which emerges of Chaucer the pilgrim from the linking passages in *The Canterbury Tales*. There is, in the Prologue to the *Man of Law's Tale*, what is almost a snide reference to Chaucer's qualities as a writer. The Man of Law, invited to contribute a story, says:

> I kan right now no thrifty tale seyn
> That Chaucer, thogh he kan but lewedly
> On metres and on rymyng craftily,
> Hath seyd hem in swich Englissh as he kan. . . .

What are we to make of this self-depreciatory reference to the author of *Troilus and Criseyde*, to mention no other of the poems? But of course Chaucer had his tongue firmly in his cheek, as if to say: How could one expect a mere lawyer to appreciate the subtleties of my prosody? Then we have the Host, Harry Bailey's account of Chaucer as a bashful, self-effacing traveller, inclined to stoutness; and the picture of himself as a tongue-tied simpleton which Chaucer puts into the mouth of the learned Eagle in *The House of Fame* (p. 45). There was a literary convention of self-depreciation commonly employed by medieval poets, but Chaucer's handling of it is, as with other conventions, individual.

Of Chaucer and the Chaucerian persona, as depicted in *The Canterbury Tales*, James Winny writes:

> The experienced man of affairs contemplates the impractical dreamer who is his complementary self and admits the incongruity by turning it to comic advantage. . . . The self-portrait offered in the poems is comically disparaging, but there is in the poetry a range and an intellectual confidence supported by an ironic discernment of truth which tells us much about the outlook and human character of its author.

This is well said, provided that we remember that Chaucer the poet, as we now know him, is based on a series of imaginative insights into his poetry by trained and perceptive readers who are more than simply textual scholars and editors. The conclusions of these readers are that there was also a man, Chaucer, a man of the world and of affairs, about whom the poet did not choose to write. We may be amused and beguiled by the picture of the naïf, self-effacing, somewhat clumsy and unprofessional poet, but we cannot for a moment accept that as a true picture of the author of Chaucer's poems. That author, we know, was a person of humanity and humour, deeply and continuously responsive to poetry as a means of self-expression, not in the confessional sense of a Romantic, but as a way of reacting to life. Chaucer was not a professional scholar, but he was very widely read. His frequent references to books and the importance of learning may certainly be taken at their face-value. Indeed, Chaucer's affirmation of the value of learning is a recurrent theme, and we can be sure that here, at least, there is no irony.

> Than mote we to bokes that we fynde,
> Thurgh whiche that olde thinges ben in mynde,
> And to the doctrine of these olde wyse,
> Yeve credence, in every skylful wise,
> That tellen of these olde appreved stories
> Of holynesse, of regnes, of victories,
> Of love, of hate, of other sondry thynges,
> Of whiche I may not maken rehersynges.
> And yf that olde bokes were aweye,
> Yloren were of remembraunce the keye.
> Wel ought us thanne honouren and beleve
> These bokes, there we han noon other preve.

Prologue to *The Legend of Good Women*, (p. 83)

Chaucer's modest hope to be numbered among the classics, despite the difficulties of writing in English, is expressed in the Envoy to *Troilus and Criseyde* (p. 80). Nor can it be doubted that the portrait of the Clerk of Oxford in the general Prologue to *The Canterbury Tales* is a sympathetic one:

> Of studie took he moost cure and moost heede.

The temptation to picture Chaucer the lover of nature and of learning was one to which a later poet yielded sympathetically. Discounting its romantic archaism, we can admit the poetically truthful insight of Longfellow's sonnet:

An old man in a lodge within a park;
The chamber walls depicted all around
With portraitures of huntsmen, hawk, and hound,
And the hurt deer. He listeneth to the lark,
Whose song comes with the sunshine through the dark
Of painted glass in leaden lattice bound;
He listeneth and he laugheth at the sound,
Then writeth in a book like any clerk.
He is the poet of the dawn, who wrote
The Canterbury Tales, and his old age
Made beautiful with song; and as I read
I hear the crowing cock, I hear the note
Of lark and linnet, and from every page
Rise odours of plough'd field or flowery mead.

This is a partial portrait, unblushingly romantic; although it leaves out Chaucer the Court official and man of affairs, in expressing a nineteenth-century poet's appreciation of another lyric and narrative poet it does something to compensate for the bareness of the historical record.

We cannot doubt that, loving literature and valuing learning as he did, Chaucer loved life more.

And as for me, though that I konne but lyte,
On bokes for to rede I me delyte,
And to hem yive I feyth and ful credence,
And in myn herte have hem in reverence
So hertely that there is game noon
That fro my bokes maketh me to goon,
But yt be seldom on the holyday,
Save, certeynly, whan that the month of May
Is comen, and that I here the foules synge,
And that the floures gynnen for to sprynge,
Farewel my bok, and my devocioun!

Prologue to *The Legend of Good Women*, (p. 83)

Yet to Chaucer books were the record and expression of life, the gateway to the experience of those long dead, the guarantee of the continuity of human existence in any intelligible aspect. In the end Chaucer the man and Chaucer the poet cannot be separated. The poetry is the essence and the proof of the man. The picture that the poems reveal is of a universal man, as Shakespeare has been called, a man concerned to regard and comment on and ultimately accept human nature in its variety; but concerned – in order to make sense of his own life amidst the human show – to make what poetry he could out of it.

III

Writing at a time of great turbulence and tension, Chaucer should appeal peculiarly to readers in a period six centuries later, when we once again seem to need, despite all the differences between our time and his, the reaffirmation of civilised values. Civilisation itself seems once again to be called in question, and the enormous fact of Chaucer and his achievement should have for us a special appeal. Yet it is not easy to bridge the apparent gap between then and now. As a middle-class man, Chaucer, it has been pointed out, by his social rise to the highest circles in the land, was in an especially favourable position to interpret society to itself. This he undertook in the great unfinished collection of tales by which he is too exclusively known. Discussing what is the specifically 'middle-class' quality of Chaucer's work, Wolfgang Clemen asks: 'Is it the sound common-sense, the compelling vigour in his manner of portrayal, his way of making "concrete" what had been "abstract", the straightforward forcefulness of the form in which certain basic truths are put before us, the preference for plain and practical workaday wisdom?'

Here, however, we are concerned, not with the *Tales*, but with his other poems, which span the whole period of his writing career, but in which his apprentice work is much in evidence. In order to write the *Tales* he had to create the medium in which they are written. In doing so he may almost be said to have created the literary tradition in English poetry – that is, the tradition from the early Tudor poets onwards. I say 'the literary tradition' because there was also a vigorous popular tradition with which he was very little concerned. I shall say nothing of this here except that it has always existed to renew and refresh the literary tradition whenever the latter has shown signs of becoming effete. The obvious instance is the renewal of poetry in the latter part of the eighteenth century by a revival of interest in the traditional ballads, partly in revolt against the gentility of the Augustan poetic establishment. Moreover, it must be said that Chaucer was never 'literary' in this effete sense. He used, evidently from love, the speech of ordinary people, enlivening the courtly vocabulary of the aristocracy with the homeliness of middle-class and popular speech. The absence of exclusive class divisions made this possible. It is partly on the basis of his language that we can claim for Chaucer the quality of universality.

If there is in the above a hint that I am falling into the practice of some literary historians of estimating Chaucer's earlier poetry by the value of its contribution to his later development, and his total achievement by what it led to in later English poetry generally, I must here disclaim any intention of offering, as a final judgement on Chaucer, what Arnold was right in calling 'the historic estimate'. Historians write with their faces to the future: poets with their faces to the past. Chaucer's greatness does not depend on the extent of his influence on later poetry. No poet writes as if he were consciously foreshadowing something that might or might not have been to come. To estimate a poet rightly we must, in the final resort, read him as if he were the *last* English poet. That is how he sees himself. Except in the case of an artist such as Milton, consciously preparing himself for some great enterprise, it is wrong to judge the earlier poems by what they led to. The only way to read Chaucer's poems that makes sense is to treat each one as an end in itself. It is the purpose of this volume to offer a choice of poems not found in the *Tales*. Even without the *Tales* Chaucer must still be regarded as, in any significant sense of the word, a major poet.

Nevertheless, his historical achievement, though it has nothing to do with the ultimate value of the poems, is of such immense importance that it must not be overlooked. In considering it, however, it must be borne in mind that the historical achievement is bound up with the poetic. The one could not have existed without the other. Nothing succeeds like success – and in Chaucer's time and literary circumstances the historical success depended on the poetic success.

Any poet, writing in England in the middle of the fourteenth century, a time when the native tongue was establishing itself over Latin and French, had several alternatives. He could write in Latin or French as the more backward-looking poets did; or he could write in the alliterative tradition, then enjoying something of a revival; or he could use the emergent tongue of the south, the language of the Court and the Universities, known as the East Midlands dialect. There was no commonly accepted English 'language', and it was by no means certain that this last variant was to be the dominant one. It was mainly Chaucer's influence that made it so, at any rate so far as poetry was concerned. By Chaucer's success the East Midlands tongue succeeded.

We shall never know precisely why the youthful Chaucer, in the mid-fourteenth century, turned his hand to poetry. No doubt he wanted to please his noble patron and entertain his circle. No doubt, too, he wished to excel in one of the expected avocations of a squire – to compose verses. Possibly he was in love and desired to please his lady. It soon became evident. either to himself or to those who encouraged him, that he had more than the ordinary talent of a court versifier. He was to do greater, more ambitious things. There was no ready-made language to hand, and no accepted English verse forms. The dreary jogtrot of the verse tale, so admirably parodied in his own *Sir Thopas*, would suit him no better than the stanzaic patterns provided by fashionable French models. He was obliged to create his own language for the poetry he wanted to write, and to take over and breathe new life into the verse forms of his French contemporaries, Machaut and Deschamps, admitted even by modern French critics to be sterile and afflicted by the *rigor mortis* of wholly artificial convention.[1] What he breathed into French forms was his own zest and humour, his own observation and freshness of outlook. Admittedly, in the works of his apprenticeship such as *The Book of the Duchess* and *The Parliament of Fowls*, he was to some extent translating. But he never translated or adapted slavishly. His was an entirely free mind. As in some degree a translator, he had an immense advantage, considering the linguistic and poetic conditions of his time and country. Poets were familiar with the conventions and traditions which governed composition throughout the Middle Ages, and it was expected that they would reverence 'authority' and make contributions of their own. There was thus a balance between tradition and innovation. While conservative poets followed tradition more or less slavishly, Chaucer took what he wanted and rejected what he saw as surplus or inimical to his poetic needs. He was writing in English for an audience which well knew the conventions of the French originals. These conventions, especially those of the dream allegory and the disputation, are referred to in the commentaries on the relevant poems at the end of this book. But what is important here is that, in rejecting this and adapting that, Chaucer was engaged in a continuous critical activity, of which the more successful and pleasing parts of his own earlier poems, uneven and unfinished as many of them are, were the witness. His business was to naturalise, but in so doing to create a viable English poetic style – a style which bears his personal and inimitable stamp. In passages from Machaut adapted in *The Book of the Duchess* there is a continuous current of critical comment, revealed not only in what Chaucer took from his originals but also in what he rejected. Fashionable poetry, in English as well as in French, was both conventional in form and

[1] Writing of Chaucer's time, Emil Legouis says: 'There never was a period in which French poetry was apparently more frail and destitute. . . . In this poor, meagre and pretentious garden there was little but artificial flowers to cull.' And again, Chaucer's main French exemplar, Guillaume de Machaut, he describes as 'one of the most debilitated of the French poets'.—Legouis and Cazamian: *A History of English Literature*, English edition, 1954.

didactic in intent, but Chaucer's need was to create a medium for the free expression of his own intelligent and humane attitude to reality, his own urge to understand, delight and entertain the world of real men and women rather than to reform and lecture to them. They liked being preached at, but this was not Chaucer's function. So in the love allegory, as typified by poems in the tradition of the *Roman de la Rose*, Chaucer strove to depict real people with real passions, not allegorical personifications. At his best he seems constitutionally incapable of not bringing an abstraction to life with some touch of realistic and graphic detail. Describing the stock personification of Avarice in his translation from the *Roman*, he writes:

> Ful foul in peyntyng was that vice;
> Ful fade and caytif was she eek,
> And also grene as ony leek.

Similarly, he turned the dream convention to his own unique uses. In medieval poetry dreams were used to invest an idea with the appearance of objective reality, presenting instruction under the guise of divine inspiration. Dreams were sent by God, as in the Old Testament, as messages on whose correct interpretation men's actions were to be based. But in using the dream framework in *The Book of the Duchess*, Chaucer introduced not instruction but a lament in very personal terms for his patron's dead wife; in describing a May morning, he turned away from conventional description to express his own love of the freshness of a summer morning, the sound of bird song and the scent of flowers.

What is to be noted in all these poems is the raciness of speech which Chaucer seems to have found it impossible to keep out of passages where we should expect him, if he were simply a conscientious translator, to have been merely formal and artificial. 'It is in your language,' he seems to be saying, 'the language of people in the street and in the market, not in that of French books, that true poetry lives. It is your thoughts and feelings, not those of the textbooks of rhetoric, that interest me and will interest my readers.' In short, though scholarship has been conscientious, sometimes to the point of tedium, in the discovery and enumeration of Chaucer's 'influences', what it has chiefly revealed, occasionally with apparent reluctance, is his almost staggering originality. When all is said and read, what above all emerges from a study of Chaucer's earlier poems is the inexplicable, the almost incredible mystery of how one man could have done so much.

Nowhere is the Chaucerian bent more striking than in his versification. Second-rate talents relied on metrical regularity and monotony, as directed by the textbooks of rhetoric. In Chaucer's handling of both the octosyllabic and the decasyllabic couplet (the latter first introduced by him into English), his 'aim', as we must call it, though it seems to have been something less conscious, is always towards freedom, towards the accommodation of free speech rhythms. He sounds like a man talking to his readers as equals and friends, or soliloquising in relaxed and meditative mood, rather than one preaching at them or exhibiting his craftsmanship. In *The House of Fame* (p. 39) he reveals, with modest self-confidence, an ironic attitude to contemporary literature and rhetoric – an attitude not found in the other writers of his day.

This much has been said about the literary and linguistic background to Chaucer's poems because an understanding of it is essential to an appreciation of his originality. We rightly reject the historic estimate; on the other hand, if we can say, as we can of Chaucer, that there was no other poet of his time writing with anything approaching his quality, and that the degree of his success could only have been achieved by a unique and historically unforeseeable genius, we pay just and undeniable tribute to his quality as a poet. In other words, in order to reject the historic estimate we need to know something of the historical background. With this, then, at the back of our minds, we can more readily appreciate the poems for themselves. Once we have, so to speak, got the poetic conventions out of the way, we find ourselves confronted with the language.

To the modern reader Chaucer is a poet writing in a language partly foreign and partly archaic: unless we are already familiar with some of his poems, therefore, we cannot approach these unfamiliar ones without being held up by difficulties of language and syntax. For this reason the poems here reprinted have been fully glossed and annotated at the end of the book. It has been assumed that in this case too much annotation is better than too little. If the poems are worth reading, they are worth understanding. Certain general considerations are worth mentioning. First, Chaucer's language must be seen as a very sensitive synthesis of native elements and the French words which had been introduced during the three centuries following the Norman Conquest. With the instinct of genius he realised that the clock could not be put back. He knew that a vigorous and durable poetic medium must make use of both the Anglo-Saxon and the Romance strain.

Chaucer wrote at a time of grammatical uncertainty, and we may find ourselves up against difficulties like that of the double negative ('Yit *nas* the ground *nat* wounded with the plough'). It is not difficult for the reader to familiarise himself with this convention, by which the negative was strengthened, not converted into a positive.

Then again, many words have completely disappeared from modern usage, and in order to understand these, recourse must be had to the notes or to the glossary. (Examples are words such as 'unnethe' – *scarcely*; 'sweven' – *dream*.) Moreover, many words have acquired different meanings in modern English (such as 'clerk' – *scholar*; 'sentence' – *meaning, opinion*). Some words, such as 'gentilesse' and 'compleccioun', are strange to us because the concepts they denote exist no longer. They belong to a medieval system of ethics or of ideas now long obsolete.

However, if the poems are read aloud as fluently as these difficulties allow, their meaning will be much clearer than if they are puzzled over in silence. The spelling is often a hindrance to immediate understanding. As John Lawlor pertinently remarks, 'Understanding of Chaucer must be based on steady recognition of the predominantly oral nature of his work.' In other words, he wrote for the ear, not for the eye. The greatest stumbling-block to the oral enjoyment of Chaucer is the final -e. This, we are told, was ceasing to exist as a pronounced syllable in the later fourteenth century. But if we treat every final -e, except before a vowel, as being sounded as a separate syllable, we shall not go far wrong. For instance, if this rule is followed in 'Tyl at the laste a larke song above', the line reads as a regular iambic pentameter. The important thing is to keep the basic rhythm in the back of the mind and to conform as closely as possible to it. I would even advocate an almost singsong rendering as a means of accustoming the ear to the sound, and thereby to the meaning, of Chaucer's lines. Moreover, I would advocate the adoption of as modern a pronunciation of the words as is compatible with their strangeness and with the rhythmic demands of the final -e. To me the adoption of a pseudo-medieval pronunciation, which has very little authority in certain knowledge (despite the persuasiveness of Professor Nevill Coghill), is a positive barrier to understanding. To my ear this makes Chaucer strange and remote, when the object should be, at least until the meaning is thoroughly grasped, to bring him as close as possible to the twentieth century without sacrificing the true Chaucerian essence.

And surely this essence is to be found in his veritable 'modernity' – the quality by which he leaps clearly out of his century and speaks to us as men and women. He speaks to us as one who loved and responded instantly to the freshness and beauty of nature and the lasting delight and instruction afforded by books; who enjoyed the comedy of manners, the perennial and indefinable fascination of women, the pathos and transcience of love, the consolations of philosophy and religion; as one who relished the absurdities of scholarly pretention and saw the need for a fresh, lively and questioning attitude to all conventions and received opinions. I have here reprinted those shorter poems and passages from long, in some cases often unfinished works, which seem to me to reveal the unique Chaucerian essence. One apology I feel is due to his spirit – I have found it impossible to give an adequate representation of his great tragi-comedy, *Troilus and Criseyde*. This is too long and too consistently good to be fairly represented except by reprinting all its five books. This was clearly impossible. But in a selection designed to show Chaucer as a lyric poet it is surely no distortion of a masterpiece to quote certain passages which stand out even in a work of such consistent excellence.

IV

A century has passed since Matthew Arnold published his famous essay *The Study of Poetry*. It is fashionable to brush aside Arnold's critical views, but he had a habit of asking the right questions, of being concerned with important issues. His views were seminal and cannot be easily or permanently disposed of. In going through the names of the great poets in search of what he regarded as 'classic' – that is, 'the best' – he examined the claims of Chaucer. His remarks are worth reconsidering, though it should be remembered that Arnold was writing of him as the author of *The Canterbury Tales*, while we are concerned principally with the other poems. Here in condensed form is what he says of Chaucer.

Having written of medieval Romance poetry, he goes on:

But in the fourteenth century there comes an Englishman nourished on this poetry, taught his trade by this poetry, getting words, rhyme, metre from this poetry; for even of that stanza which the Italians used, and which Chaucer derived immediately from the Italians, the basis and suggestion was probably given in France. . . . Chaucer's power of fascination, however, is enduring; his poetical importance does not need the assistance of the historic estimate; it is real. He is a genuine source of joy and strength, which is flowing still for us and will flow always. . . .

And yet Chaucer is not one of the great classics. His poetry transcends and effaces, easily and without effort, all the romance-poetry of Catholic Christendom . . . something is wanting . . . to the poetry of Chaucer, which poetry must have before it can be placed in the glorious class of the best. And there is no doubt what that something is. It is the σπομδαιότης, the high and excellent seriousness, which Aristotle assigns as one of the grand virtues of poetry. The substance of Chaucer's poetry, his view of things and his criticism of life, has largeness, freedom, shrewdness, benignity; but it has not this high seriousness. Homer's criticism of life has it, Dante's has it, Shakespeare's has it.

Arnold has previously quoted eight lines from *The Prioress's Tale* in which the murdered boy tells of his murder:

My throte is cut unto my nekke-bone . . .

He has also previously quoted the single line:

O martir souded to virginitee.

Arnold has some just things to say of Chaucer's view of life. He clearly values and enjoys the *Tales*, but it must be doubted whether his estimate was really more than historic, despite his protestations to the contrary. He tells us that Chaucer's value is 'real', not merely historic, but his comments are essentially comparative: Chaucer was better than all the other medieval Romance poets, but he did not have the high seriousness of Homer, of Dante, of Shakespeare. It has been pointed out that Arnold was the victim of his 'touchstone' theory of poetic value, according to which he quotes certain lines of poetry from Homer, Milton, Shakespeare and Dante, in order to place other poetry beside them and see if it stands up to the test. It has also been pointed out that his 'touchstones' ('Absent thee from felicity awhile' – Shakespeare; and 'In la sua volontade è nostra pace' – Dante, etc.) were nearly all expressive of stoic resignation in the face of ineluctable fate. It is notable that even his line from Chaucer – the nearest he can get to a touchstone – is expressive of stoic resignation: 'O martir souded to virginitee'. In short, although Arnold elsewhere eschews a didactic view of poetry, he really wants poetry to moralise, to preach, to be what religion was failing to be at the time he wrote. If you have a pre-conceived notion of what constitutes the classic 'best', based on the view of Aristotle, a non-poet, you are going to find it hard to react to a poet for what he is, rather than for what he fails to be.

Some critics have always wanted to think of Shakespeare as the supreme moralist. There can be no case for this. Cartloads of books have failed to discover and enunciate Shakespeare's moral principles. As a dramatist he wanted to see life whole, to observe, to hold the mirror up to nature, to show men and women what they were like, in both their private and their public capacities. So with Chaucer. He too was a dramatic poet, observing, commenting on society, holding the mirror up to medieval life in its complexity, its variety, its multifarious and jostling humanity. If we admit, as Arnold does, that Chaucer's view of life is shrewd, large, free, how can we deny him seriousness, even though his criticism of life is comic in spirit? We need name only Molière or Cervantes to illustrate the truth that comedy can be of the utmost seriousness. It can be admitted, without disparagement, that Arnold was inclined to overdo the importance of seriousness in its more obvious sense. Not only must a poet's criticism of life, he seems to be saying, be serious, it must be seen to be serious. It must sound a note of solemn rhetoric. This is where he sometimes went wrong in his own poetry. Chaucer is not Homer, Dante, Shakespeare or Milton. He is himself, and his observation of humanity, his insight into its passions and weaknesses, its virtues and strengths, is unique.

Nevertheless, although we may regret the limiting effect of Arnold's insistence on a kind of focused high seriousness, a condensation of moral nobility into single lines, we are entitled to expect that the best poetry, in which it is now, a hundred years after Arnold, acceptable to include Chaucer, shall come to a head, so to speak, to gather at certain points into a concentration of poetic expressiveness. We expect to find brief passages, stanzas, lines, where there has been a drawing together of verbal energy rising above the more diffused and general level of the poet's work. If a poet is good in extended passages, there are likely to be brief lyrics or single strokes in which he is as good or even better. Without quoting from *The Canterbury Tales* or going outside the selections in this volume, it is not hard to find passages in which Chaucer excels. Once a reader habituates himself to the vocabulary and rhythm of the verse, he will recognise in such lines as these from

Anelida and Arcite a tone which had never before been heard in English poetry and which was to become permanent.

> Be favorable eke thou Polymya,
> On Parnaso that with thy sustres glade,
> By Elycon not fer from Cirrea,
> Singest with vois memorial in the shade . . .

'Singest with vois memorial in the shade': the same accent is to be heard from Spenser to Milton and later. Notice that Chaucer has hit on the combination of Germanic and Romance words which Shakespeare has in the *Hamlet* passage quoted by Arnold. Just as

> If ever thou didst hold me in thy heart,
> Absent thee from felicity awhile . . .

exploits the complementary qualities of the two main sources of English, so Chaucer's line complements the dignity of the Romance 'vois memorial' with the Germanic concreteness of 'singest' and 'shade'.

Perhaps we should be wrong in attributing high seriousness in Arnold's sense to such a passage as this. But can it be denied to these lines from the ballade entitled *Truth*?

> That thee is sent, receyve in buxumnesse;
> The wrastling for this world axeth a fal.
> Her is non hoom, her nis but wildernesse:
> Forth, pilgrim, forth! Forth, beste, out of thy stal!
> Know thy contree, look up, thank God of al;
> Hold the heye wey, and lat thy gost thee lede;
> And trouthe thee shal delivere, it is no drede.

Or again, take the opening lines of *The Parliament of Fowls*:

> The lyf so short, the craft so long to lerne,
> Th'assay so hard, so sharp the conquerynge,
> The dredful joye, alwey that slit so yerne,
> Al this mene I by Love . . .

There is something about this reflection on what was to become the major theme of Chaucer's poetry – love – which is scarcely matched anywhere outside Shakespeare.

Surely the opening of the ballade in the Prologue to *The Legend of Good Women* strikes for the first time the note of high rhetoric which was to echo again and again until at least the end of the nineteenth century.

> Hyd, Absolon, thy gilte tresses clere;
> Ester, ley thou thy meknesse al adown;
> Hyd, Jonathas, al thy frendly manere;
> Penalopee and Marcia Catoun,
> Make of youre wifhod no comparysoun;
> Hyde ye youre beautes, Ysoude and Eleyne:
> My lady cometh, that al this may disteyne.

If Arnold is right in not discerning in Chaucer the kind of stoical determinism he looked for, and which his own poetry, at its most characteristic, seeks to reproduce, he was surely lacking in breadth of poetic and human sympathy in not responding to a tone which occurs throughout *Troilus and Criseyde*, a tone of profound and tender pity for the transitoriness of love and youth.

> O yonge, fresshe folkes, he or she,
> In which that love upgroweth with youre age,
> Repeyreth hom fro worldly vanyte,
> And of youre herte up casteth the visage
> To thilke God that after his ymage
> Yow made, and thynketh al nys but a faire
> This world, that passeth soone as floures faire.

There is here something of a philosophical commonplace: the world's vanity was a recurrent theme of medieval religious speculation. But if the subject-matter of these lines is a commonplace, does not the expression invest it with a freshness and a pathos which make the thought new?

One of the most touchingly pathetic stanzas in *Troilus and*

Criseyde is that in which Pandarus reflects privately on the sorrow he knows to be in store for Troilus when Criseyde fails, as the older man knows she will fail, to keep her promise and return to Troy.

> Pandare answerde, 'It may be, wel ynough,'
> And held with hym of al that evere he seyde.
> But in his herte he thoughte, and softe lough,
> And to hymself ful sobreliche he seyde,
> 'From haselwode, there joly Robin pleyde,
> Shal come al that that thow abidest heere.
> Ye, fare wel al the snow of ferne yere!'

Here the pathos is touched with irony in a manner unexcelled outside Chaucer, even in Shakespeare. The lines come at a focal point in the story, and must be read in their context for the full impact to be felt. That the pathos of Troilus' lot is given utterance by the worldly ironist is a master-stroke of narrative-dramatic creation, for it raises the situation above the level of Troilus' passionate expressions of romantic love and grief and distances it from the immediacy of ephemeral emotion.

Such writing as this lifts Chaucer above all merely historical considerations and gives him the status of a classic, if there is any meaning in this term. If the reader is encouraged to familiarise himself with Chaucer's vocabulary and syntax – so hard at first the assay – so as to be able to read him as easily as he reads Spenser or Milton, he will have extended the range of his poetic understanding and enjoyment by a century and a half.

J. R.

Lewes 1970

SELECT BIBLIOGRAPHY

COMPLETE EDITION

The Works of Geoffrey Chaucer, edited by F. N. Robinson, second edition, Oxford, 1957

BIOGRAPHICAL AND CRITICAL

Hussey, Spearing and Winny, *An Introduction to Chaucer*, Cambridge, 1965

J. Livingston Lowes, *Geoffrey Chaucer*, Indiana University Press, 1934

J. M. Manly, *Some New Light on Chaucer*, Bell, 1926

John Lawlor, *Chaucer*, Hutchinson, 1968

Wolfgang Clemen, *Chaucer's Early Poetry*, Methuen, 1963

from *The Romaunt of the Rose*

The Dream

Within my twenty yer of age,	21
Whan that Love taketh his cariage	
Of yonge folk, I wente soone	
To bedde, as I was wont to done,	
And faste I slepte; and in slepyng	25
Me mette such a swevenyng	
That lyked me wonders wel.	
But in that sweven is never a del	
That it nys afterward befalle,	
Ryght as this drem wol tel us alle.	30
Now this drem wol I ryme aright	
To make your hertes gaye and lyght,	
For Love it prayeth, and also	
Commaundeth me that it be so.	
And if there any aske me,	35
Whether that it be he or she,	
How this book, [the] which is here,	
Shal hatte, that I rede you here:	
It is the Romance of the Rose,	
In which al the art of love I close.	40
The mater fayre is of to make;	
God graunt me in gree that she it take	
For whom that it begonnen is!	
And that is she that hath, ywis,	
So mochel pris; and therto she	45

So worthy is biloved to be,
That she wel ought, of pris and ryght,
Be cleped Rose of every wight.
    That it was May me thoughte tho—
It is fyve yer or more ago— 50
That it was May, thus dremed me,
In tyme of love and jolite,
That al thing gynneth waxen gay,
For ther is neither busk nor hay
In May, that it nyl shrouded ben, 55
And it with newe leves wren.
These wodes eek recoveren grene,
That drie in wynter ben to sene;
And the erthe wexith proud withalle,
For swote dewes that on it falle, 60
And the pore estat forget
In which that wynter had it set.
And than bycometh the ground so proud
That it wole have a newe shroud,
And makith so queynt his robe and faire 65
That it hath hewes an hundred payre
Of gras and flouris, ynde and pers,
And many hewes ful dyvers.
That is the robe I mene, iwis,
Through which the ground to preisen is. 70
    The byrdes that han left her song,
While thei suffride cold so strong,
In wedres gryl and derk to sighte,
Ben in May, for the sonne brighte,
So glade that they shewe in syngyng 75
That in her hertis is sich lykyng
That they mote syngen and be light.
Than doth the nyghtyngale hir myght
To make noyse and syngen blythe.
Than is blisful many sithe 80

26

The chelaundre and papyngay.
Than yonge folk entenden ay
Forto ben gay and amorous,
The tyme is than so saverous.
Hard is the hert that loveth nought   85
In May, whan al this mirth is wrought,
Whan he may on these braunches here
The smale briddes syngen clere
Her blisful swete song pitous.
And in this sesoun delytous,   90
Whan love affraieth alle thing,
Me thought a-nyght, in my sleping,
Right in my bed, ful redily,
That it was by the morowe erly,
And up I roos, and gan me clothe.   95
Anoon I wissh myn handis bothe;
A sylvre nedle forth y drough
Out of an aguler queynt ynough,
And gan this nedle threde anon;
For out of toun me list to gon   100
The song of briddes forto here,
That in thise buskes syngen clere.
And in the swete seson that leef is,
With a thred bastyng my slevis,
Alone I wente in my plaiyng,   105
The smale foules song harknyng,
That peyned hem, ful many peyre,
To synge on bowes blosmed feyre.
Jolif and gay, ful of gladnesse,
Toward a ryver gan I me dresse,   110
That I herd renne faste by;
For fairer plaiyng non saugh I
Than playen me by that ryver.
For from an hill that stood ther ner,
Cam doun the strem ful stif and bold.   115

27

Cleer was the water, and as cold
As any welle is, soth to seyne;
And somdel lasse it was than Seyne,
But it was strayghter wel away.
And never saugh I, er that day,   120
The watir that so wel lyked me;
And wondir glad was I to se
That lusty place and that ryver.
And with that watir, that ran so cler,
My face I wyssh. Tho saugh I well   125
The botme paved everydell
With gravel, ful of stones shene.
The medewe softe, swote and grene,
Beet right on the watir syde.
Ful cler was than the morowtyde,   130
And ful attempre, out of drede.
    Tho gan I walke thorough the mede,
Dounward ay in my pleiyng,
The ryver syde costeiyng.

The Garden

And whan I had a while goon,   135
I saugh a gardyn right anoon,
Ful long and brood, and everydell
Enclosed was, and walled well
With highe walles enbatailled,
Portraied without and wel entailled   140
With many riche portraitures.
And bothe the ymages and peyntures
Gan I biholde bysyly;
And I wole telle you redyly
Of thilk ymages the semblaunce,   145
As fer as I have in remembraunce.

Amydde saugh I Hate stonde,
That for hir wrathe, yre, and onde,
Semede to ben a moveresse,
An angry wight, a chideresse;   150
And ful of gyle and fel corage,
By semblaunt, was that ilk ymage.
And she was nothyng wel arraied,
But lyk a wod womman afraied.
Yfrounced foule was hir visage,   155
And grennyng for dispitous rage;
Hir nose snorted up for tene.
Ful hidous was she for to sene,
Ful foul and rusty was she, this.
Hir heed ywrithen was, ywis,   160
Ful grymly with a greet towayle.   161

Avarice

Another ymage set saugh I   207
Next Coveitise faste by,
And she was clepid Avarice.
Ful foul in peyntyng was that vice;   210
Ful fade and caytif was she eek,
And also grene as ony leek.
So yvel hewed was hir colour,
Hir semed to have lyved in langour.
She was lyk thyng for hungre deed,   215
That ladde hir lyf oonly by breed
Kneden with eisel strong and egre,
And therto she was lene and megre.
And she was clad ful porely
Al in an old torn courtepy,   220

As she were al with doggis torn;
And bothe bihynde and eke biforn
Clouted was she beggarly.
A mantyl heng hir faste by,
Upon a perche, weik and small;   225
A burnet cote heng therwithall
Furred with no menyver,
But with a furre rough of her,
Of lambe-skynnes hevy and blake;
It was ful old, I undirtake.   230
For Avarice to clothe hir well
Ne hastith hir never a dell;
For certeynly it were hir loth
To weren ofte that ilke cloth;
And if it were forwered, she   235
Wolde have ful gret necessite
Of clothyng, er she bought hir newe,
Al were it bad of woll and hewe.
This Avarice hild in hir hand
A purs that heng [doun] by a band,   240
And that she hidde and bond so stronge,
Men must abyde wondir longe
Out of that purs er ther come ought.
For that ne cometh not in hir thought;
It was not, certein, hir entente   245
That fro that purs a peny wente.   246

from *The Book of the Duchess*

The Dream

Me thoghte thus: that hyt was May,   291
And in the dawenynge I lay
(Me mette thus) in my bed al naked,
And loked forth, for I was waked
With smale foules a gret hep   295
That had affrayed me out of my slep,
Thorgh noyse and swetnesse of her song.
And, as me mette, they sate among
Upon my chambre roof wythoute,
Upon the tyles, overal aboute,   300
And songen, everych in hys wyse,
The moste solempne servise
By noote, that ever man, y trowe,
Had herd; for som of hem song lowe,
Som high, and al of oon acord.   305
To telle shortly, att oo word.
Was never herd so swete a steven,—
But hyt had be a thyng of heven,—
So mery a soun, so swete entewnes,
That certes, for the toun of Tewnes,   310
I nolde but I had herd hem synge;
For al my chambre gan to rynge
Thurgh syngynge of her armonye.
For instrument nor melodye
Was nowhere herd yet half so swete,   315

Nor of acord half so mete;
For ther was noon of hem that feyned
To synge, for ech of hem hym peyned
To fynde out mery crafty notes.
They ne spared not her throtes.   320
And sooth to seyn, my chambre was
Ful wel depeynted, and with glas
Were al the wyndowes wel yglased,
Ful clere, and nat an hoole ycrased,
That to beholde hyt was gret joye.   325
For holly al the story of Troye
Was in the glasynge ywroght thus,
Of Ector and of kyng Priamus,
Of Achilles and Lamedon,
And eke of Medea and of Jason,   330
Of Paris, Eleyne, and of Lavyne.
And alle the walles with colours fyne
Were peynted, bothe text and glose,
Of al the Romaunce of the Rose.
My wyndowes were shette echon,   335
And throgh the glas the sonne shon
Upon my bed with bryghte bemes,
With many glade gilde stremes;
And eke the welken was so fair,—
Blew, bryght, clere was the ayr,   340
And ful attempre for sothe hyt was;
For nother to cold nor hoot yt nas,
Ne in al the welken was no clowde.
    And as I lay thus, wonder lowde
Me thoght I herde an hunte blowe   345
T'assay hys horn, and for to knowe
Whether hyt were clere or hors of soun.
And I herde goynge, bothe up and doun,
Men, hors, houndes, and other thyng;
And al men speken of huntyng,   350

How they wolde slee the hert with strengthe,
And how the hert had, upon lengthe,
So moche embosed, y not now what.
    Anoon ryght, whan I herde that,
How that they wolde on-huntynge goon,   355
I was ryght glad, and up anoon
Took my hors, and forth I wente
Out of my chambre; I never stente
Til I com to the feld withoute.
Ther overtok y a gret route   360
Of huntes and eke of foresteres,
With many relayes and lymeres,
And hyed hem to the forest faste
And I with hem. So at the laste
I asked oon, ladde a lymere: 365
'Say, felowe, who shal hunte here?'
Quod I, and he answered ageyn,
'Syr, th'emperour Octovyen,'
Quod he, 'and ys here faste by.'
'A Goddes half, in good tyme!' quod I,   370
'Go we faste!' and gan to ryde.
Whan we came to the forest syde,
Every man dide ryght anoon
As to huntynge fil to doon.
The mayster-hunte anoon, fot-hot,   375
With a gret horn blew thre mot
At the uncouplynge of hys houndes.
Withynne a while the hert yfounde ys,
Yhalowed, and rechased faste
Longe tyme; and so at the laste   380
This hert rused, and staal away
Fro alle the houndes a privy way.
The houndes had overshote hym alle,
And were on a defaute yfalle.
Therwyth the hunte wonder faste   385

Blew a forloyn at the laste.
  I was go walked fro my tree,
And as I wente, ther cam by mee
A whelp, that fauned me as I stood,
That hadde yfolowed, and koude no good.   390
Hyt com and crepte to me as lowe
Ryght as hyt hadde me yknowe,
Helde doun hys hed and joyned hys eres,
And leyde al smothe doun hys heres.
I wolde have kaught hyt, and anoon   395
Hyt fledde, and was fro me goon;
And I hym folwed, and hyt forth wente
Doun by a floury grene wente
Ful thikke of gras, ful softe and swete.
With floures fele, faire under fete,   400
And litel used, hyt semed thus;
For both Flora and Zephirus,
They two that make floures growe,
Had mad her dwellynge ther, I trowe;
For hit was, on to beholde,   405
As thogh the erthe envye wolde
To be gayer than the heven,
To have moo floures, swiche seven,
As in the welken sterres bee.
Hyt had forgete the povertee   410
That wynter, thorgh hys colde morwes,
Had mad hyt suffre, and his sorwes,
All was forgeten, and that was sene.
For al the woode was waxen grene;
Swetnesse of dew had mad hyt waxe.   415

Complaint of the Black Knight against Fortune

No man may my sorwe glade,   563
That maketh my hewe to falle and fade,

And hath myn understondynge lorn,   565
That me ys wo that I was born!
May noght make my sorwes slyde,
Nought al the remedyes of Ovyde,
Ne Orpheus, god of melodye,
Ne Dedalus with his playes slye;   570
Ne hele me may no phisicien,
Noght Ypocras, ne Galyen;
Me ys wo that I lyve houres twelve.
But whooso wol assay hymselve
Whether his hert kan have pitee   575
Of any sorwe, lat hym see me.
Y wreche, that deth hath mad al naked
Of al the blysse that ever was maked,
Yworthe worste of alle wyghtes,
That hate my dayes and my nyghtes!   580
My lyf, my lustes, be me loothe,
For al welfare and I be wroothe.
The pure deth ys so ful my foo
That I wolde deye, hyt wolde not soo;
For whan I folwe hyt, hit wol flee;   585
I wolde have hym, hyt nyl nat me.
This ys my peyne wythoute red,
Alway deynge and be not ded,
That Cesiphus, that lyeth in helle,
May not of more sorwe telle,   590
And whoso wiste al, by my trouthe,
My sorwe, but he hadde rowthe
And pitee of my sorwes smerte,
That man hath a fendly herte;
For whoso seeth me first on morwe   595
May seyn he hath met with sorwe,
For y am sorwe, and sorwe ys y.
    'Allas! and I wol tel the why:
My song ys turned to pleynynge,

35

And al my laughtre to wepynge,   600
My glade thoghtes to hevynesse;
In travayle ys myn ydelnesse
And eke my reste; my wele is woo,
My good ys harm, and evermoo
In wrathe ys turned my pleynge   605
And my delyt into sorwynge.
Myn hele ys turned into seknesse,
In drede ys al my sykernesse;
To derke ys turned al my lyght,
My wyt ys foly, my day ys nyght,   610
My love ys hate, my slep wakynge,
My myrthe and meles ys fastynge,
My countenaunce ys nycete,
And al abaved, where so I be;
My pees, in pledynge and in werre.   615
Allas! how myghte I fare werre?
My boldnesse ys turned to shame,
For fals Fortune hath pleyd a game
Atte ches with me, allas the while!
The trayteresse fals and ful of gyle,   620
That al behoteth, and nothyng halt,
She goth upryght and yet she halt,
That baggeth foule and loketh faire,
The dispitouse debonaire,
That skorneth many a creature!   625
An ydole of fals portrayture
Ys she, for she wol sone wrien;
She is the monstres hed ywrien,
As fylthe over-ystrawed with floures.
Hir moste worshippe and hir flour ys   630
To lyen, for that ys hyr nature;
Withoute feyth, lawe, or mesure
She ys fals; and ever laughynge
With oon eye, and that other wepynge.

That ys broght up, she set al doun.   635
I lykne hyr to the scorpioun,
That ys a fals, flaterynge beste;
For with his hed he maketh feste,
But al amydde hys flaterynge
With hys tayle he wol stynge   640
And envenyme; and so wol she.
She ys th'envyouse charite
That ys ay fals, and semeth wel,
So turneth she hyr false whel
Aboute, for hyt ys nothyng stable,   645
Now by the fire, now at table;
For many oon hath she thus yblent.
She ys pley of enchauntement,
That semeth oon and ys not soo.
The false thef! what hath she doo,   650
Trowest thou? By oure Lord I wol the seye.
At the ches with me she gan to pleye;
With hir false draughtes dyvers
She staal on me, and tok my fers.
And whan I sawgh my fers awaye,   655
Allas! I kouthe no lenger playe,
But seyde, "Farewel, swete, ywys,
And farewel al that ever ther ys!"
Therwith Fortune seyde "Chek her!"
And "Mat!" in myd poynt of the chekker,   660
With a poun errant, allas!
Ful craftier to pley she was
Than Athalus, that made the game
First of the ches, so was hys name.
But God wolde I had oones or twyes   665
Ykoud and knowe the jeupardyes
That kowde the Grek Pithagores!
I shulde have pleyed the bet at ches,
And kept my fers the bet therby.

And thogh wherto? for trewely   670
I holde that wyssh nat worth a stree!
Hyt had be never the bet for me.
For Fortune kan so many a wyle,
Ther be but fewe kan hir begile,
And eke she ys the lasse to blame;   675
Myself I wolde have do the same,
Before God, hadde I ben as she;
She oghte the more excused be.
For this I say yet more therto,
Had I be God and myghte have do   680
My wille, whan she my fers kaughte,
I wolde have drawe the same draughte.
For, also wys God yive me reste,
I dar wel swere she took the beste.
But through that draughte I have lorn   685
My blysse; allas! that I was born!
For evermore, y trowe trewly,
For al my wille, my lust holly
Ys turned; but yet, what to doone?
Be oure Lord, hyt ys to deye soone.   690
For nothyng I leve hyt noght,
But lyve and deye ryght in this thoght;
For there nys planete in firmament,
Ne in ayr ne in erthe noon element,
That they ne yive me a yifte echone   695
Of wepynge whan I am allone.
For whan that I avise me wel,
And bethenke me every del,
How that ther lyeth in rekenyng,
In my sorwe, for nothyng;   700
And how ther leveth no gladnesse
May glade me of my distresse,
And how I have lost suffisance,
And therto I have no plesance,

Than may I say I have ryght noght.   705
And whan al this falleth in my thoght,
Allas! than am I overcome!
For that ys doon ys not to come.
I have more sorowe than Tantale.'   709

from *The House of Fame*

Book I

'And therefore Joves, thorgh hys grace,   661
Wol that I bere the to a place
Which that hight the Hous of Fame,
To do the som disport and game,
In som recompensacion   665
Of labour and devocion,
That thou hast had, loo causeles,
To Cupido, the rechcheles!
And thus this god, thorgh his merite,
Wol with som maner thing the quyte,   670
So that thou wolt be of good chere.
For truste wel that thou shalte here,
When we be come there I seye,
Mo wonder thynges, dar I leye,
And of Loves folk moo tydynges,   675
Both sothe sawes and lesinges;
And moo loves newe begonne,
And longe yserved loves wonne,
And moo loves casuelly
That ben betyd, no man wot why,   680
But as a blynd man stert an hare;

And more jolytee and fare,
While that they fynde love of stel,
As thinketh hem, and over-al wel;
Mo discordes, moo jelousies,   685
Mo murmures, and moo novelries,
And moo dissymulacions,
And feyned reparacions;
And moo berdys in two houres
Withoute rasour or sisoures   690
Ymad, then greynes be of sondes;
And eke moo holdynge in hondes,
And also moo renovelaunces
Of olde forleten aqueyntaunces;
Mo love-dayes and acordes   695
Then on instrumentes be cordes;
And eke of loves moo eschaunges
Then ever cornes were in graunges,—
Unnethe maistow trowen this?'
Quod he. 'Noo, helpe me God so wys!'   700
Quod I. 'Noo? why?' quod he. 'For hyt
Were impossible, to my wit,
Though that Fame had alle the pies
In al a realme, and alle the spies,
How that yet she shulde here al this,   705
Or they espie hyt.' 'O yis, yis!'
Quod he to me, 'that kan I preve
Be reson worthy for to leve,
So that thou yeve thyn advertence
To understonde my sentence.   710
    'First shalt thou here where she duelleth,
And so thyn oune bok hyt tellith;
Hir paleys stant, as I shal seye,
Ryght even in myddes of the weye
Betwixen hevene, erthe, and see;   715
That what so ever in al these three

Is spoken, either privy or apert,
The way therto ys so overt,
And stant eke in so juste a place
That every soun mot to hyt pace,   720
Or what so cometh from any tonge,
Be hyt rouned, red, or songe,
Or spoke in suerte or in drede,
Certeyn, hyt moste thider nede.

   'Now herkene wel, for-why I wille   725
Tellen the a propre skille
And a worthy demonstracion
In myn ymagynacion.

   'Geffrey, thou wost ryght wel this,
That every kyndely thyng that is   730
Hath a kyndely stede ther he
May best in hyt conserved be;
Unto which place every thyng,
Thorgh his kyndely enclynyng,
Moveth for to come to,   735
Whan that hyt is awey therfro;
As thus: loo, thou maist alday se
That any thing that hevy be,
As stoon, or led, or thyng of wighte,
And bere hyt never so hye on highte,   740
Lat goo thyn hand, hit falleth doun.
Ryght so seye I be fyr or soun,
Or smoke, or other thynges lyghte;
Alwey they seke upward on highte.
While ech of hem is at his large,   745
Lyght thing upward, and dounward charge.
And for this cause mayst thou see
That every ryver to the see
Enclyned ys to goo by kynde,
And by these skilles, as I fynde,   750
Hath fyssh duellynge in flood and see,

41

And treës eke in erthe bee.
Thus every thing, by thys reson,
Hath his propre mansyon,
To which hit seketh to repaire,   755
Ther-as hit shulde not apaire.
Loo, this sentence ys knowen kouth
Of every philosophres mouth,
As Aristotle and daun Platon,
And other clerkys many oon;   760
And to confirme my resoun,
Thou wost wel this, that spech is soun,
Or elles no man myghte hyt here;
Now herke what y wol the lere.
    'Soun ys noght but eyr ybroken,   765
And every speche that ys spoken,
Lowd or pryvee, foul or fair,
In his substaunce ys but air;
For as flaumbe ys but lyghted smoke,
Ryght soo soun ys air ybroke.   770
But this may be in many wyse,
Of which I will the twoo devyse,
As soun that cometh of pipe or harpe.
For whan a pipe is blowen sharpe,
The air ys twyst with violence   775
And rent; loo, thys ys my sentence;
Eke, whan men harpe-strynges smyte,
Whether hyt be moche or lyte,
Loo, with the strok the ayr tobreketh;
And ryght so breketh it when men speketh.   780
Thus wost thou wel what thing is speche.
    'Now hennesforth y wol the teche
How every speche, or noyse, or soun,
Thurgh hys multiplicacioun,
Thogh hyt were piped of a mous,   785
Mot nede come to Fames Hous.

I preve hyt thus—take hede now—
Be experience; for yf that thow
Throwe on water now a stoon,
Wel wost thou, hyt wol make anoon   790
A litel roundell as a sercle,
Paraunter brod as a covercle;
And ryght anoon thow shalt see wel,
That whel wol cause another whel,
And that the thridde, and so forth, brother,   795
Every sercle causynge other
Wydder than hymselve was;
And thus fro roundel to compas,
Ech aboute other goynge
Causeth of othres sterynge   800
And multiplyinge ever moo,
Til that hyt be so fer ygoo,
That hyt at bothe brynkes bee.
Although thou mowe hyt not ysee
Above, hyt gooth yet alway under,   805
Although thou thenke hyt a gret wonder.
And whoso seyth of trouthe I varye,
Bid hym proven the contrarye.
And ryght thus every word, ywys,
That lowd or pryvee spoken ys,   810
Moveth first an ayr aboute,
And of thys movynge, out of doute,
Another ayr anoon ys meved,
As I have of the watir preved,
That every cercle causeth other.   815
Ryght so of ayr, my leve brother;
Everych ayr another stereth
More and more, and speche up bereth,
Or voys, or noyse, or word, or soun,
Ay through multiplicacioun,   820
Til hyt be atte Hous of Fame,—

Take yt in ernest or in game.
    'Now have I told, yf thou have mynde,
How speche or soun, of pure kynde,
Enclyned ys upward to meve;   825
This, mayst thou fele, wel I preve.
And that same place, ywys,
That every thyng enclyned to ys,
Hath his kyndelyche stede:
That sheweth hyt, withouten drede,   830
That kyndely the mansioun
Of every speche, of every soun,
Be hyt eyther foul or fair,
Hath hys kynde place in ayr.
And syn that every thyng that is   835
Out of hys kynde place, ywys,
Moveth thidder for to goo,
Yif hyt aweye be therfroo,
As I have before preved the,
Hyt seweth, every soun, parde,   840
Moveth kyndely to pace
Al up into his kyndely place.
And this place of which I telle,
Ther as Fame lyst to duelle,
Ys set amyddys of these three,   845
Heven, erthe, and eke the see,
As most conservatyf the soun.
Than ys this the conclusyoun,
That every speche of every man,
As y the telle first began,   850
Moveth up on high to pace
Kyndely to Fames place.
    'Telle me this now feythfully,
Have y not preved thus symply,
Withoute any subtilite   855
Of speche, or gret prolixite

44

Of termes of philosophie,
Of figures of poetrie,
Or colours of rethorike?
Pardee, hit oughte the to lyke!   860
For hard langage and hard matere
Ys encombrous for to here
Attones; wost thou not wel this?'
And y answered and seyde, 'Yis.'
    'A ha!' quod he, 'lo, so I can   865
Lewedly to a lewed man
Speke, and shewe hym swyche skiles
That he may shake hem be the biles,
So palpable they shulden be.
But telle me this, now praye y the,   870
How thinketh the my conclusyon?'
[Quod he]. 'A good persuasion,'
Quod I, 'hyt is; and lyk to be
Ryght so as thou hast preved me.'
'Be God,' quod he, 'and as I leve,   875
Thou shalt have yet, or hit be eve,
Of every word of thys sentence
A preve by experience,
And with thyne eres heren wel
Top and tayl, and everydel,   880
That every word that spoken ys
Cometh into Fames Hous, ywys,
As I have seyd; what wilt thou more?'
And with this word upper to sore
He gan, and seyde, 'Be seynt Jame,   885
Now wil we speken al of game!'   886

Anelida and Arcite

The Compleynt of feire Anelida and fals Arcite

Invocation

Thou ferse god of armes, Mars the rede,
That in the frosty contre called Trace,
Within thy grisly temple ful of drede
Honoured art, as patroun of that place;
With thy Bellona, Pallas, ful of grace,   5
Be present, and my song contynue and guye;
At my begynnyng thus to the I crye.

For hit ful depe is sonken in my mynde,
With pitous hert in Englyssh to endyte
This olde storie, in Latyn which I fynde,   10
Of quene Anelida and fals Arcite,
That elde, which that al can frete and bite,
As hit hath freten mony a noble storie,
Hath nygh devoured out of oure memorie.

Be favorable eke, thou Polymya,   15
On Parnaso that with thy sustres glade,
By Elycon, not fer from Cirrea,
Singest with vois memorial in the shade,
Under the laurer which that may not fade,
And do that I my ship to haven wynne.   20
First folowe I Stace, and after him Corynne.

46

The Story

Iamque domos patrias Cithice post aspera gentis
Prelia laurigero subeunte Thesea curru
Letifici plausus missusque ad sidera vulgi

When Theseus, with werres longe and grete,
The aspre folk of Cithe had overcome,
With laurer corouned, in his char gold-bete,
Hom to his contre-houses is he come;   25
For which the peple, blisful al and somme,
So cryëden that to the sterres hit wente,
And him to honouren dide al her entente.

Beforn this duk, in signë of victorie,
The trompes come, and in his baner large   30
The ymage of Mars; and, in token of glorie,
Men myghte sen of tresour many a charge,
Many a bright helm, and many a spere and targe,
Many a fresh knyght, and many a blysful route,
On hors, on fote, in al the feld aboute.   35

Ipolita his wif, the hardy quene
Of Cithia, that he conquered hadde,
With Emelye, her yonge suster shene,
Faire in a char of gold he with him ladde,
That al the ground about her char she spradde   40
With brightnesse of the beaute in her face,
Fulfilled of largesse and of alle grace.

With his tryumphe, and laurer-corouned thus,
In al the flour of Fortunes yevynge,
Let I this noble prince Theseus   45
Toward Athenes in his wey rydinge,
And founde I wol in shortly for to bringe

47

The slye wey of that I gan to write,
Of quene Anelida and fals Arcite.

Mars, which that through his furious cours of ire,   50
The olde wrathe of Juno to fulfille,
Hath set the peples hertes bothe on fire
Of Thebes and Grece, everich other to kille
With blody speres, ne rested never stille,
But throng now her, now ther, among hem bothe,   55
That everych other slough, so were they wrothe.

For when Amphiorax and Tydeus,
Ipomedon, Parthonope also
Were ded, and slayn proude Campaneus,
And when the wrecched Thebans, bretheren two,   60
Were slayn, and kyng Adrastus hom ago,
So desolat stod Thebes and so bare,
That no wight coude remedie of his care.

And when the olde Creon gan espye
How that the blood roial was broght a-doun,   65
He held the cite by his tyrannye,
And dyde the gentils of that regioun
To ben his frendes, and dwellen in the toun.
So, what for love of him, and what for awe,
The noble folk were to the toun idrawe.   70

Among al these Anelida, the quene
Of Ermony, was in that toun dwellynge,
That fairer was then is the sonne shene.
Thurghout the world so gan her name springe,
That her to seen had every wyght likynge;   75
For, as of trouthe, is ther noon her lyche,
Of al the women in this worlde riche.

Yong was this quene, of twenty yer of elde,
Of mydel stature, and of such fairenesse,
That Nature had a joye her to behelde;   80
And for to speken of her stidfastnesse,
She passed hath Penelope and Lucresse;
And shortly, yf she shal be comprehended,
In her ne myghte no thing been amended.

This Theban knyght [Arcite] eke, soth to seyn,   85
Was yong, and therwithal a lusty knyght,
But he was double in love and no thing pleyn,
And subtil in that craft over any wyght,
And with his kunnyng wan this lady bryght;
For so ferforth he gan her trouthe assure   90
That she him trusted over any creature.

What shuld I seyn? she loved Arcite so
That when that he was absent any throwe,
Anon her thoghte her herte brast a-two.
For in her sight to her he bar hym lowe,   95
So that she wende have al his hert yknowe;
But he was fals; hit nas but feyned chere,—
As nedeth not to men such craft to lere.

But nevertheles ful mykel besynesse
Had he, er that he myghte his lady wynne,   100
And swor he wolde dyen for distresse,
Or from his wit he seyde he wolde twynne.
Alas, the while! for hit was routhe and synne,
That she upon his sorowes wolde rewe;
But nothing thinketh the fals as doth the trewe.   105

Her fredom fond Arcite in such manere
That al was his that she hath, moche or lyte;
Ne to no creature made she chere

Ferther then that hit lyked to Arcite.
Ther nas no lak with which he myghte her wite: 110
She was so ferforth yeven hym to plese,
That al that lyked hym hit dyde her ese.

Ther nas to her no maner lettre sent
That touched love, from any maner wyght,
That she ne shewed hit him, er hit was brent;   115
So pleyn she was, and dide her fulle myght
That she nyl hiden nothing from her knyght,
Lest he of any untrouthe her upbreyde.
Withoute bode his heste she obeyde.

And eke he made him jelous over here,   120
That what that any man had to her seyd,
Anoon he wolde preyen her to swere
What was that word, or make him evel apaid.
Then wende she out of her wyt have breyd;
But al this nas but sleght and flaterie;   125
Without love, he feyned jelousye.

And al this tok she so debonerly,
That al his wil, her thoghte hit skilful thing;
And ever the lenger she loved him tendirly,
And dide him honour as he were a kyng.   130
Her herte was to him wedded with a ring;
So ferforth upon trouthe is her entente,
That wher he gooth, her herte with him wente.

When she shal ete, on him is so her thoght,
That wel unnethe of mete tok she kep;   135
And when that she was to her reste broght,
On him she thoghte alwey til that she slep;
When he was absent, prevely she wep:

Thus lyveth feire Anelida the quene
For fals Arcite, that dide her al this tene.   140

This fals Arcite, of his newfanglenesse,
For she to him so lowly was and trewe,
Tok lesse deynte of her stidfastnesse,
And saw another lady, proud and newe,
And ryght anon he cladde him in her hewe—   145
Wot I not whethir in white, rede, or grene—
And falsed fair Anelida the quene.

But neverthelesse, gret wonder was hit noon
Thogh he were fals, for hit is kynde of man,
Sith Lamek was, that is so longe agoon,   150
To ben in love as fals as evere he can;
He was the firste fader that began
To loven two, and was in bigamye;
And he found tentes first, but yf men lye.

This fals Arcite, sumwhat moste he feyne,   155
When he wex fals, to covere his traitorie,
Ryght as an hors, that can both bite and pleyne;
For he bar her on honde of trecherie,
And swor he coude her doublenesse espie,
And al was falsnes that she to him mente.   160
Thus swor this thef, and forth his way he wente.

Alas! what herte myght enduren hit,
For routhe or wo, her sorwe for to telle?
Or what man hath the cunnyng or the wit?
Or what man mighte within the chambre dwelle,   165
Yf I to him rehersen sholde the helle
That suffreth fair Anelida the quene
For fals Arcite, that dide her al this tene.

She wepith, waileth, swowneth pitously;
To grounde ded she falleth as a ston; 170
Craumpyssheth her lymes crokedly;
She speketh as her wit were al agon;
Other colour then asshen hath she noon;
Non other word speketh she, moche or lyte,
But 'merci, cruel herte myn, Arcite!' 175

And thus endureth, til that she was so mat
That she ne hath foot on which she may sustene;
But forth languisshing evere in this estat,
Of which Arcite hath nouther routhe ne tene.
His herte was elleswhere, newe and grene, 180
That on her wo ne deyneth him not to thinke;
Him rekketh never wher she flete or synke.

His newe lady holdeth him so narowe
Up by the bridil, at the staves ende,
That every word he dredeth as an arowe; 185
Her daunger made him bothe bowe and bende,
And as her liste, made him turne or wende;
For she ne graunted him in her lyvynge
No grace, whi that he hath lust to singe,

But drof hym forth, unnethe liste her knowe 190
That he was servaunt unto her ladishippe;
But lest that he were proud, she held him lowe.
Thus serveth he, withoute fee or shipe;
She sent him now to londe, now to shippe;
And for she yaf him daunger al his fille, 195
Therfor she hadde him at her owne wille.

Ensample of this, ye thrifty wymmen alle,
Take her of Anelida and Arcite,
That for her liste him 'dere herte' calle,

And was so meke, therfor he loved her lyte.   200
The kynde of mannes herte is to delyte
In thing that straunge is, also God me save!
For what he may not gete, that wolde he have.

Now turne we to Anelida ageyn,
That pyneth day be day in langwisshinge;   205
But when she saw that her ne gat no geyn,
Upon a day, ful sorowfully wepinge,
She caste her for to make a compleynynge,
And with her owne hond she gan hit write,
And sente hit to her Theban knyght, Arcite.   210

The compleynt of Anelida the quene upon fals Arcite

Proem

So thirleth with the poynt of remembraunce
The swerd of sorowe, ywhet with fals plesaunce,
Myn herte, bare of blis and blak of hewe,
That turned is in quakyng al my daunce,
My surete in awhaped countenaunce,   215
Sith hit availeth not for to ben trewe;
For whoso trewest is, hit shal hir rewe,
That serveth love and doth her observaunce
Alwey til oon, and chaungeth for no newe.

Strophe

1.

I wot myself as wel as any wight;   220
For I loved oon with al myn herte and myght,
More then myself an hundred thousand sithe,

And called him myn hertes lif, my knyght,
And was al his, as fer as hit was ryght;
And when that he was glad, then was I blithe,   225
And his disese was my deth as swithe;
And he ayein his trouthe hath me plyght
Fo evermore, his lady me to kythe.

2.

Now is he fals, alas! and causeles,
And of my wo he is so routheles,   230
That with a word him list not ones deyne
To bringe ayen my sorowful herte in pes,
For he is caught up in another les.
Ryght as him list, he laugheth at my peyne,
And I ne can myn herte not restreyne,   235
For to love him alwey neveretheles;
And of al this I not to whom me pleyne.

3.

And shal I pleyne—alas! the harde stounde—
Unto my foo that yaf myn herte a wounde,
And yet desireth that myn harm be more?   240
Nay, certis, ferther wol I never founde
Non other helpe, my sores for to sounde.
My destinee hath shapen hit so ful yore;
I wil non other medecyne ne lore;
I wil ben ay ther I was ones bounde.   245
That I have seid, be seid for evermore!

4.

Alas! wher is become your gentilesse,
Youre wordes ful of plesaunce and humblesse,

Youre observaunces in so low manere,
And your awayting and your besynesse   250
Upon me, that ye calden your maistresse,
Your sovereyne lady in this world here?
Alas! is ther now nother word ne chere
Ye vouchen sauf upon myn hevynesse?
Alas! youre love, I bye hit al to dere.   255

5.

Now, certis, swete, thogh that ye
Thus causeles the cause be
Of my dedly adversyte,
Your manly resoun oghte hit to respite,
To slen your frend, and namely me,   260
That never yet in no degre
Offended yow, as wisly he,
That al wot, out of wo my soule quyte!
But for I shewed yow, Arcite,
Al that men wolde to me write,   265
And was so besy yow to delyte—
Myn honor save—meke, kynde, and fre,
Therfor ye put on me this wite.
Alas! ye rekke not a myte,
Thogh that the swerd of sorwe byte   270
My woful herte through your cruelte.

6.

My swete foo, why do ye so, for shame?
And thenke ye that furthered be your name
To love a newe, and ben untrewe? Nay!
And putte yow in sclaunder now and blame,   275
And do to me adversite and grame,
That love yow most—God, wel thou wost—alway?

55

Yet come ayein, and yet be pleyn som day,
And than shal this, that now is mys, be game,
And al foryive, while that I lyve may.   280

Antistrophe

1.

Lo! herte myn, al this is for to seyne,
As whether shal I preye or elles pleyne?
Which is the wey to doon yow to be trewe?
For either mot I have yow in my cheyne,
Or with the deth ye mote departe us tweyne;   285
Ther ben non other mene weyes new.
For God so wisly upon my soule rewe,
As verrayly ye sleen me with the peyne;
That may ye se unfeyned on myn hewe.

2.

For thus ferforth have I my deth [y-]soght,   290
Myself I mordre with my privy thoght;
For sorowe and routhe of your unkyndenesse
I wepe, I wake, I faste; al helpeth noght;
I weyve joye that is to speke of oght,
I voyde companye, I fle gladnesse.   295
Who may avaunte her beter of hevynesse
Then I? And to this plyte have ye me broght,
Withoute gilt,—me nedeth no witnesse.

3.

And shal I preye, and weyve womanhede?
Nay! rather deth then do so foul a dede!   300

And axe merci, gilteles,—what nede?
And yf I pleyne what lyf that I lede,
Yow rekketh not; that knowe I, out of drede;
And if that I to yow myne othes bede
For myn excuse, a skorn shal be my mede.   305
Your chere floureth, but it wol not sede;
Ful longe agoon I oghte have taken hede.

4.

For thogh I hadde yow to-morowe ageyn,
I myghte as wel holde Aperill fro reyn,
As holde yow, to make yow be stidfast.   310
Almyghty God, of trouthe sovereyn,
Wher is the trouthe of man? Who hath hit slayn?
Who that hem loveth, she shal hem fynde as fast
As in a tempest is a roten mast.
Is that a tame best that is ay feyn   315
To renne away, when he is lest agast?

5.

Now merci, swete, yf I mysseye!
Have I seyd oght amys, I preye?
I noot; my wit is al aweye.
I fare as doth the song of *Chaunte-pleure*;   320
For now I pleyne, and now I pleye,
I am so mased that I deye;
Arcite hath born awey the keye
Of al my world, and my good aventure.
For in this world nis creature   325
Wakynge, in more discomfiture
Than I, ne more sorowe endure.
And yf I slepe a furlong wey or tweye,
Then thynketh me that your figure

Before me stont, clad in asure,   330
To profren eft a newe asure
For to be trewe, and merci me to preye.

6.

The longe nyght this wonder sight I drye,
And on the day for thilke afray I dye,
And of al this ryght noght, iwis, ye reche.   335
Ne nevere mo myn yen two be drie,
And to your routhe, and to your trouthe, I crie.
But welawey! to fer be they to feche;
Thus holdeth me my destinee a wreche.
But me to rede out of this drede, or guye,   340
Ne may my wit, so weyk is hit, not streche.

Conclusion

Then ende I thus, sith I may do no more,—
I yeve hit up for now and evermore;
For I shal never eft putten in balaunce
My sekernes, ne lerne of love the lore.   345
But as the swan, I have herd seyd ful yore,
Ayeins his deth shal singen his penaunce,
So singe I here my destinee or chaunce,
How that Arcite Anelida so sore
Hath thirled with the poynt of remembraunce.   350

The Story continued

When that Anelida, this woful quene,
Hath of her hand ywriten in this wise,
With face ded, betwixe pale and grene,

She fel a-swowe; and sith she gan to rise,
And unto Mars avoweth sacrifise   355
Withinne the temple, with a sorowful chere,
That shapen was as ye shal after here.

[*Unfinished*]

from *The Parliament of Fowls*

The lyf so short, the craft so long to lerne,
Th'assay so hard, so sharp the conquerynge,
The dredful joye, alwey that slit so yerne:
Al this mene I by Love, that my felynge
Astonyeth with his wonderful werkynge   5
So sore, iwis, that whan I on hym thynke,
Nat wot I wel wher that I flete or synke.

For al be that I knowe nat Love in dede,
Ne wot how that he quiteth folk here hyre,
Yit happeth me ful ofte in bokes reede   10
Of his myrakles and his crewel yre.
There rede I wel he wol be lord and syre;
I dar nat seyn, his strokes been so sore,
But 'God save swich a lord!'—I can na moore.

Of usage—what for lust and what for lore—   15
On bokes rede I ofte, as I yow tolde.
But wherfore that I speke al this? Nat yoore
Agon, it happede me for to beholde
Upon a bok, was write with lettres olde,

And therupon, a certeyn thing to lerne,   20
The longe day ful faste I redde and yerne.

For out of olde feldes, as men seyth,
Cometh al this newe corn from yer to yere,
And out of olde bokes, in good feyth,
Cometh al this newe science that men lere.   25
But now to purpos as of this matere;
To rede forth hit gan me so delite,
That al that day me thoughte but a lyte.

This bok of which I make mencioun
Entitled was al thus as I shal telle: 30
'Tullyus of the Drem of Scipioun.'
Chapitres sevene it hadde, of hevene and helle
And erthe, and soules that therinne dwelle,
Of whiche, as shortly as I can it trete,
Of his sentence I wol yow seyn the greete.   35

Fyrst telleth it, whan Scipion was come
In Affrike, how he meteth Massynisse,
That hym for joie in armes hath inome;
Thanne telleth it here speche and al the blysse
That was betwix hem til the day gan mysse,   40
And how his auncestre, Affrycan so deere,
Gan in his slep that nyght to hym apere.

Thanne telleth it that, from a sterry place,
How Affrycan hath hym Cartage shewed,
And warnede hym beforn of al his grace,   45
And seyde hym what man, lered other lewed
That lovede commune profyt, wel ithewed,
He shulde into a blysful place wende,
There as joye is that last withouten ende.

Thanne axede he if folk that here been dede   50
Han lyf and dwellynge in another place.
And Affrican seyde, 'Ye, withouten drede,'
And that oure present worldes lyves space
Nis but a maner deth, what wey we trace,
And rightful folk shul gon, after they dye,   55
To hevene; and shewede hym the Galaxye.

Thanne shewede he hym the lytel erthe that here is,
At regard of the hevenes quantite;
And after shewede he hym the nyne speres,
And after that the melodye herde he   60
That cometh of thilke speres thryes thre,
That welle is of musik and melodye
In this world here, and cause of armonye.

Than bad he hym, syn erthe was so lyte,
And ful of torment and of harde grace,   65
That he ne shulde hym in the world delyte.
Thanne tolde he hym, in certeyn yeres space
That every sterre shulde come into his place
Ther it was first, and al shulde out of mynde
That in this world is don of al mankynde.   70

Thanne preyede hym Scipion to telle hym al
The wey to come into that hevene blisse.
And he seyde, 'Know thyself first immortal,
And loke ay besyly thow werche and wysse
To commune profit, and thow shalt not mysse   75
To comen swiftly to that place deere
That ful of blysse is and of soules cleere.

'But brekers of the lawe, soth to seyne,
And likerous folk, after that they ben dede,
Shul whirle aboute th'erthe alwey in peyne,   80

Tyl many a world be passed, out of drede,
And than, foryeven al hir wikked dede,
Than shul they come into this blysful place,
To which to comen God the sende his grace.'

The day gan faylen, and the derke nyght,   85
That reveth bestes from here besynesse,
Berafte me my bok for lak of lyght,
And to my bed I gan me for to dresse,
Fulfyld of thought and busy hevynesse;
For bothe I hadde thyng which that I nolde,   90
And ek I nadde that thyng that I wolde.

But fynally, my spirit at the laste,
For wery of my labour al the day,
Tok reste, that made me to slepe faste,
And in my slep I mette, as that I lay,   95
How Affrican, ryght in the selve aray
That Scipion hym say byfore that tyde,
Was come and stod right at my beddes syde.

The wery huntere, slepynge in his bed,
To wode ayeyn his mynde goth anon;   100
The juge dremeth how his plees been sped;
The cartere dremeth how his cartes gon;
The riche, of gold; the knyght fyght with his fon;
The syke met he drynketh of the tonne;
The lovere met he hath his lady wonne.   105

Can I not seyn if that the cause were
For I hadde red of Affrican byforn,
That made me to mete that he stod there;
But thus seyde he: 'Thow hast the so wel born
In lokynge of myn olde bok totorn,   110

Of which Macrobye roughte nat a lyte,
That sumdel of thy labour wolde I quyte.'

Cytherea! thow blysful lady swete,
That with thy fyrbrond dauntest whom the lest,
And madest me this sweven for to mete,   115
Be thow myn helpe in this, for thow mayst best!
As wisly as I sey the north-north-west,
Whan I began my sweven for to write,
So yif me myght to ryme and ek t'endyte!

This forseyde Affrican me hente anon,   120
And forth with hym unto a gate broughte,
Ryght of a park walled with grene ston,
And over the gate, with lettres large iwroughte,
There were vers iwriten, as me thoughte,
On eyther half, of ful gret difference,   125
Of which I shal now seyn the pleyn sentence:

'Thorgh me men gon into that blysful place
Of hertes hele and dedly woundes cure;
Thorgh me men gon unto the welle of grace,
There grene and lusty May shal evere endure.   130
This is the wey to al good aventure.
Be glad, thow redere, and thy sorwe of-caste;
Al open am I—passe in, and sped thee faste!'

'Thorgh me men gon,' than spak that other side,
'Unto the mortal strokes of the spere   135
Of which Disdayn and Daunger is the gyde,
Ther nevere tre shal fruyt ne leves bere.
This strem yow ledeth to the sorweful were
There as the fish in prysoun is al drye;
Th'eschewing is only the remedye!'   140

These vers of gold and blak iwriten were,
Of whiche I gan astoned to beholde,
For with that oon encresede ay my fere,
And with that other gan myn herte bolde;
That oon me hette, that other dide me colde: 145
No wit hadde I, for errour, for to chese,
To entre or flen, or me to save or lese.

Right as, betwixen adamauntes two
Of evene myght, a pece of yren set
Ne hath no myght to meve to ne fro—   150
For what that oon may hale, that other let—
Ferde I, that nyste whether me was bet
To entre or leve, til Affrycan, my gide,
Me hente, and shof in at the gates wide,

And seyde, 'It stondeth writen in thy face,   155
Thyn errour, though thow telle it not to me;
But dred the not to come into this place,
For this writyng nys nothyng ment bi the,
Ne by non, but he Loves servaunt be:
For thow of love hast lost thy tast, I gesse,   160
As sek man hath of swete and bytternesse.

'But nathales, although that thow be dul,
Yit that thow canst not do, yit mayst thow se.
For many a man that may nat stonde a pul,
It liketh hym at the wrastlyng for to be,   165
And demeth yit wher he do bet or he.
And if thow haddest connyng for t'endite,
I shal the shewe mater of to wryte.'

With that myn hand in his he tok anon,
Of which I confort caughte, and wente in faste.   170
But, Lord, so I was glad and wel begoon!

64

For overal where that I myne eyen caste
Were treës clad with leves that ay shal laste,
Ech in his kynde, of colour fresh and greene
As emeraude, that joye was to seene.   175

The byldere ok, and ek the hardy asshe;
The piler elm, the cofre unto carayne;
The boxtre pipere, holm to whippes lashe;
The saylynge fyr; the cipresse, deth to playne;
The shetere ew; the asp for shaftes pleyne;   180
The olyve of pes, and eke the dronke vyne;
The victor palm, the laurer to devyne.

A gardyn saw I ful of blosmy bowes
Upon a ryver, in a grene mede,
There as swetnesse everemore inow is,   185
With floures white, blewe, yelwe, and rede,
And colde welle-stremes, nothyng dede,
That swymmen ful of smale fishes lighte,
With fynnes rede and skales sylver bryghte.

On every bow the bryddes herde I synge,   190
With voys of aungel in here armonye;
Some besyede hem here bryddes forth to brynge;
The litel conyes to here pley gonne hye;
And ferther al aboute I gan aspye
The dredful ro, the buk, the hert and hynde,   195
Squyrels, and bestes smale of gentil kynde.

Of instruments of strenges in acord
Herde I so pleye a ravyshyng swetnesse,
That God, that makers is of al and lord,
Ne herde nevere beter, as I gesse.   200
Therwith a wynd, unnethe it myghte be lesse,

Made in the leves grene a noyse softe
Acordaunt to the foules song alofte.

Th'air of that place so attempre was
That nevere was ther grevaunce of hot ne cold;   20
There wex ek every holsom spice and gras;
No man may there waxe sek ne old;
Yit was there joye more a thousandfold
Than man can telle; ne nevere wolde it nyghte,
But ay cler day to any manes syghte.   210

Under a tre, besyde a welle, I say
Cupide, oure lord, his arwes forge and file;
And at his fet his bowe al redy lay;
And Wille, his doughter, temprede al this while
The hevedes in the welle, and with hire file   21
She touchede hem, after they shulde serve
Some for to sle, and some to wounde and kerve.

Tho was I war of Plesaunce anon-ryght,
And of Aray, and Lust, and Curteysie,
And of the Craft that can and hath the myght   220
To don by force a wyght to don folye—
Disfigurat was she, I nyl nat lye;
And by hymself, under an ok, I gesse,
Saw I Delyt, that stod with Gentilesse.

I saw Beute withouten any atyr,   225
And Youthe, ful of game and jolyte;
Foolhardynesse, Flaterye, and Desyr,
Messagerye, and Meede, and other thre—
Here names shul not here be told for me—
And upon pilers greete of jasper longe   230
I saw a temple of bras ifounded stronge.

Aboute that temple daunseden alwey
Women inowe, of whiche some ther weere
Fayre of hemself, and some of hem were gay;
In kertels, al dishevele, wente they there: 235
That was here offyce alwey, yer by yeere.
And on the temple, of dowves white and fayre
Saw I syttynge many an hundred peyre.

Before the temple-dore ful soberly
Dame Pees sat, with a curtyn in hire hond,   240
And by hire syde, wonder discretly,
Dame Pacience syttynge there I fond,
With face pale, upon an hil of sond;
And aldernext, withinne and ek withoute,
Byheste and Art, and of here folk a route.   245

Withinne the temple, of sykes hoote as fyr
I herde a swogh that gan aboute renne,
Whiche sikes were engendered with desyr,
That maden every auter for to brenne
Of newe flaume, and wel espyed I thenne   250
That al the cause of sorwes that they drye
Cam of the bittere goddesse Jelosye.

The god Priapus saw I, as I wente,
Withinne the temple in sovereyn place stonde,
In swich aray as whan the asse hym shente   255
With cri by nighte, and with hys sceptre in honde.
Ful besyly men gonne assaye and fonde
Upon his hed to sette, of sondry hewe,
Garlondes ful of freshe floures newe.

And in a prive corner in disport   260
Fond I Venus and hire porter Richesse,
That was ful noble and hautayn of hyre port.

Derk was that place, but afterward lightnesse
I saw a lyte, unnethe it myghte be lesse,
And on a bed of gold she lay to reste,   265
Til that the hote sonne gan to weste.

Hyre gilte heres with a golden thred
Ibounden were, untressed as she lay,
And naked from the brest unto the hed
Men myghte hire sen; and, sothly for to say,   270
The remenaunt was wel kevered to my pay,
Ryght with a subtyl coverchef of Valence—
Ther nas no thikkere cloth of no defense.

The place yaf a thousand savours sote,
And Bachus, god of wyn, sat hire besyde,   275
And Ceres next, that doth of hunger boote,
And, as I seyde, amyddes lay Cypride,
To whom on knees two yonge folk ther cryde
To ben here helpe. But thus I let hire lye,
And ferther in the temple I gan espie   280

That, in dispit of Dyane the chaste,
Ful many a bowe ibroke heng on the wal
Of maydenes swiche as gonne here tymes waste
In hyre servyse; and peynted overal
Of many a story, of which I touche shal   285
A fewe, as of Calyxte and Athalante,
And many a mayde of which the name I wante.

Semyramis, Candace, and Hercules,
Biblis, Dido, Thisbe, and Piramus,
Tristram, Isaude, Paris, and Achilles,   290
Eleyne, Cleopatre, and Troylus,
Silla, and ek the moder of Romulus:

Alle these were peynted on that other syde,
And al here love, and in what plyt they dyde.

Whan I was come ayeyn into the place   295
That I of spak, that was so sote and grene,
Forth welk I tho myselven to solace.
Tho was I war wher that ther sat a queene
That, as of lyght the somer sonne shene
Passeth the sterre, right so over mesure   300
She fayrer was than any creature.

And in a launde, upon an hil of floures,
Was set this noble goddesse Nature.
Of braunches were here halles and here boures
Iwrought after here cast and here mesure;   305
Ne there nas foul that cometh of engendrure
That they ne were prest in here presence,
To take hire dom and yeve hire audyence.

For this was on seynt Valentynes day,
Whan every foul cometh there to chese his make,   310
Of every kynde that men thynke may,
And that so huge a noyse gan they make
That erthe, and eyr, and tre, and every lake
So ful was, that unethe was there space
For me to stonde, so ful was al the place.   315

And right as Aleyn, in the Pleynt of Kynde,
Devyseth Nature of aray and face,
In swich aray men myghte hire there fynde.
This noble emperesse, ful of grace,
Bad every foul to take his owne place,   320
As they were woned alwey fro yer to yeere,
Seynt Valentynes day, to stonden theere.

That is to seyn, the foules of ravyne
Weere hyest set, and thanne the foules smale
That eten, as hem Nature wolde enclyne,   325
As worm or thyng of which I telle no tale;
And water-foul sat lowest in the dale;
But foul that lyveth by sed sat on the grene,
And that so fele that wonder was to sene.

There myghte men the royal egle fynde,   330
That with his sharpe lok perseth the sonne,
And othere egles of a lowere kynde,
Of whiche that clerkes wel devyse conne.
Ther was the tiraunt with his fetheres donne
And grey, I mene the goshauk, that doth pyne   335
To bryddes for his outrageous ravyne.

The gentyl faucoun, that with his feet distrayneth
The kynges hand; the hardy sperhauk eke,
The quayles foo; the merlioun, that payneth
Hymself ful ofte the larke for to seke;   340
There was the douve with hire yën meke;
The jelous swan, ayens his deth that syngeth;
The oule ek, that of deth the bode bryngeth;

The crane, the geaunt, with his trompes soun;
The thef, the chough, and ek the janglynge pye;   345
The skornynge jay; the eles fo, heroun;
The false lapwynge, ful of trecherye;
The stare, that the conseyl can bewrye;
The tame ruddok, and the coward kyte;
The kok, that orloge is of thorpes lyte;   350

The sparwe, Venus sone; the nyghtyngale,
That clepeth forth the grene leves newe;
The swalwe, mortherere of the foules smale

That maken hony of floures freshe of hewe;
The wedded turtil, with hire herte trewe;   355
The pekok, with his aungels fetheres bryghte;
The fesaunt, skornere of the cok by nyghte;

The waker goos; the cukkow ever unkynde;
The popynjay, ful of delicasye;
The drake, stroyere of his owene kynde;   360
The stork, the wrekere of avouterye;
The hote cormeraunt of glotenye;
The raven wys; the crowe with vois of care;
The throstil old; the frosty feldefare.

What shulde I seyn? Of foules every kynde   365
That in this world han fetheres and stature
Men myghten in that place assembled fynde
Byfore the noble goddesse of Nature,
And everich of hem dide his besy cure
Benygnely to chese or for to take,   370
By hire acord, his formel or his make.   371

Now Welcome Summer

And whan this werk al brought was to an ende,   666
To every foul Nature yaf his make
By evene acord, and on here way they wende.
And, Lord, the blisse and joye that they make!
For ech of hem gan other in wynges take,   670
And with here nekkes ech gan other wynde,
Thankynge alwey the noble goddesse of kynde.

But fyrst were chosen foules for to synge,
As yer by yer was alwey hir usaunce
To synge a roundel at here departynge,   675
To don to Nature honour and plesaunce.

71

The note, I trowe, imaked was in Fraunce,
The wordes were swiche as ye may heer fynde,
The nexte vers, as I now have in mynde.

'Now welcome, somer, with thy sonne softe,   680
That hast this wintres wedres overshake,
And driven away the longe nyghtes blake!

'Saynt Valentyn, that art ful hy on-lofte,
Thus syngen smale foules for thy sake:
Now welcome, somer, with thy sonne softe,   685
That hast this wintres wedres overshake.

'Wel han they cause for to gladen ofte,
Sith ech of hem recovered hath hys make,
Ful blissful mowe they synge when they wake:
Now welcome, somer, with thy sonne softe,   690
That hast this wintres wedres overshake,
And driven away the longe nyghtes blake!'

And with the shoutyng, whan the song was do
That foules maden at here flyght awey,
I wok, and othere bokes tok me to,   695
To reede upon, and yit I rede alwey.
I hope, ywis, to rede so som day
That I shal mete som thyng for to fare
The bet, and thus to rede I nyl nat spare.   699

from *Troilus and Criseyde*

Book II Criseyde's Dream

The dayes honour, and the hevenes yë,   904
The nyghtes foo—al this clepe I the sonne—
Gan westren faste, and downward for to wrye,
As he that hadde his dayes cours yronne;
And white thynges wexen dymme and donne
For lak of lyght, and sterres for t'apere,
That she and alle hire folk in went yfeere.   910

So whan it liked hire to go to reste,
And voided weren thei that voiden oughte,
She seyde that to slepen wel hire leste.
Hire wommen soone til hire bed hire broughte.
Whan al was hust, than lay she stille and thoughte   915
Of al this thing; the manere and the wise
Reherce it nedeth nought, for ye ben wise.

A nyghtyngale, upon a cedir grene,
Under the chambre wal ther as she ley,
Ful loude song ayein the moone shene,   920
Peraunter, in his briddes wise, a lay
Of love, that made hire herte fressh and gay.
That herkned she so longe in good entente,
Til at the laste the dede slep hire hente.

And as she slep, anonright tho hire mette   925
How that an egle, fethered whit as bon,

Under hire brest his longe clawes sette,
And out hire herte he rente, and that anon,
And dide his herte into hire brest to gon,
Of which she nought agroos, ne nothyng smerte;   930
And forth he fleigh, with herte left for herte.   931

Book III Pandarus and Criseyde

Pandare, o-morwe which that comen was   1555
Unto his nece and gan hire faire grete,
Seyde, 'Al this nyght so reyned it, allas,
That al my drede is that ye, nece swete,
Han litel laiser had to slepe and mete.
Al nyght,' quod he, 'hath reyn so do me wake,   1560
That som of us, I trowe, hire hedes ake.'

And ner he com, and seyde, 'How stant it now
This mury morwe? Nece, how kan ye fare?'
Criseyde answerde, 'Nevere the bet for yow,
Fox that ye ben! God yeve youre herte kare!   1565
God help me so, ye caused al this fare,
Trowe I,' quod she, 'for al youre wordes white.
O, whoso seeth yow, knoweth yow ful lite.'

With that she gan hire face for to wrye
With the shete, and wax for shame al reed;   1570
And Pandarus gan under for to prie,
And seyde, 'Nece, if that I shal be ded,
Have here a swerd and smyteth of myn hed!'
With that his arm al sodeynly he thriste
Under hire nekke, and at the laste hire kyste.   1575

Book V Troilus and Criseyde Parted

Upon the walles faste ek wolde he walke,   666
And on the Grekis oost he wolde se,

And to hymself right thus he wolde talke:
'Lo, yonder is myn owene lady free,
Or ellis yonder, ther the tentes be.   670
And thennes comth this eyr, that is so soote,
That in my soule I fele it doth me boote.

'And hardily this wynd, that more and moore
Thus stoundemele encresseth in my face,
Is of my ladys depe sikes soore.   675
I preve it thus, for in noon othere place
Of al this town, save onliche in this space,
Fele I no wynd that sowneth so lik peyne:
It seyth, "Allas! whi twynned be we tweyne?" '

This long tyme he dryveth forth right thus,   680
Til fully passed was the nynthe nyght;
And ay bisyde hym was this Pandarus,
That bisily did al his fulle myght
Hym to conforte, and make his herte light,
Yevyng hym hope alwey, the tenthe morwe   685
That she shal come, and stynten al his sorwe.

Upon that other syde ek was Criseyde,
With wommen fewe, among the Grekis stronge;
For which ful ofte a day 'Allas!' she seyde,
'That I was born! Wel may myn herte longe   690
After my deth; for now lyve I to longe.
Allas! and I ne may it nat amende!
For now is wors than evere yet I wende.

'My fader nyl for nothyng do me grace
To gon ayeyn, for naught I kan hym queme;   695
And if so be that I my terme pace,
My Troilus shal in his herte deme
That I am fals, and so it may wel seme:

75

Thus shal ich have unthonk on every side.
That I was born, so weilaway the tide!   700

'And if that I me putte in jupartie,
To stele awey by nyght, and it bifalle
That I be kaught, I shal be holde a spie;
Or elles—lo, this drede I moost of alle—
If in the hondes of som wrecche I falle,   705
I nam but lost, al be myn herte trewe.
Now, myghty God, thow on my sorwe rewe!'

Ful pale ywoxen was hire brighte face,
Hire lymes lene, as she that al the day
Stood, whan she dorste, and loked on the place   710
Ther she was born, and ther she dwelt hadde ay;
And al the nyght wepying, allas, she lay.
And thus despeired, out of alle cure,
She ladde hire lif, this woful creature.   714

Book V Troilus and Pandarus

The laurer-crowned Phebus, with his heete,   1107
Gan, in his course ay upward as he wente,
To warmen of the est see the wawes weete,
And Nysus doughter song with fressh entente,   1110
Whan Troilus his Pandare after sente;
And on the walles of the town they pleyde,
To loke if they kan sen aught of Criseyde.

Tyl it was noon, they stoden for to se
Who that ther come; and every maner wight   1115
That com fro fer, they seyden it was she,
Til that thei koude knowen hym aright.
Now was his herte dul, now was it light.

And thus byjaped stonden for to stare
Aboute naught this Troilus and Pandare.   1120

To Pandarus this Troilus tho seyde,
'For aught I woot, byfor noon, sikirly,
Into this town ne comth nat here Criseyde.
She hath ynough to doone, hardyly,
To wynnen from hire fader, so trowe I.   1125
Hire olde fader wol yet make hire dyne
Er that she go; God yeve hys herte pyne!'

Pandare answerede, 'It may wel be, certeyn.
And forthi lat us dyne, I the byseche,
And after noon than maystow come ayeyn.'   1130
And hom they go, withoute more speche,
And comen ayeyn; but longe may they seche
Er that they fynde that they after gape.
Fortune hem bothe thenketh for to jape!

Quod Troilus, 'I se wel now that she   1135
Is taried with hire olde fader so,
That er she come, it wol neigh even be.
Com forth, I wole unto the yate go.
Thise porters ben unkonnyng evere mo,
And I wol don hem holden up the yate   1140
As naught ne were, although she come late.'

The day goth faste, and after that com eve,
And yet com nought to Troilus Criseyde.
He loketh forth by hegge, by tre, by greve,
And fer his hed over the wal he leyde,   1145
And at the laste he torned hym and seyde,
'By God, I woot hire menyng now, Pandare!
Almoost, ywys, al newe was my care.

'Now douteles, this lady kan hire good;
I woot, she meneth riden pryvely.   1150
I commende hire wisdom, by myn hood!
She wol nat maken peple nycely
Gaure on hire whan she comth; but softely
By nyghte into the town she thenketh ride.
And, deere brother, thynk not longe t'abide.   1155

'We han naught elles for to don, ywis.
And Pandarus, now woltow trowen me?
Have here my trouthe, I se hire! yond she is!
Heve up thyn eyen, man! maistow nat se?'
Pandare answerede, 'Nay, so mote I the!   1160
Al wrong, by God! What saistow, man, where arte?
That I se yond nys but a fare-carte.'

'Allas! thow seyst right soth,' quod Troilus.
'But, hardily, it is naught al for nought
That in myn herte I now rejoysse thus.   1165
It is ayeyns som good I have a thought.
Not I nat how, but syn that I was wrought,
Ne felte I swich a comfort, dar I seye;
She comth to-nyght, my lif that dorste I leye!'

Pandare answerede, 'It may be, wel ynough,'   1170
And held with hym of al that evere he seyde.
But in his herte he thoughte, and softe lough,
And to hymself ful sobreliche he seyde,
'From haselwode, there joly Robyn pleyde,
Shal come al that that thow abidest heere.   1175
Ye, fare wel al the snow of ferne yere!'   1176

Litera Criseydis

'Cupides sone, ensample of goodlyheede,   1590
O swerd of knyghthod, sours of gentilesse,
How myght a wight in torment and in drede
And heleles, yow sende as yet gladnesse?
I herteles, I sik, I in destresse!
Syn ye with me, nor I with yow, may dele,   1595
Yow neyther sende ich herte may nor hele.

'Youre lettres ful, the papir al ypleynted,
Conceyved hath myn hertes pietee.
I have ek seyn with teris al depeynted
Youre lettre, and how that ye requeren me   1600
To come ayeyn, which yet ne may nat be.
But whi, lest that this lettre founden were,
No mencioun ne make I now, for feere.

'Grevous to me, God woot, is youre unreste,
Youre haste, and that the goddes ordinaunce   1605
It semeth nat ye take it for the beste.
Nor other thyng nys in youre remembraunce,
As thynketh me, but only youre plesaunce.
But beth nat wroth, and that I yow biseche;
For that I tarie is al for wikked speche.   1610

'For I have herd wel moore than I wende,
Touchyng us two, how thynges han ystonde;
Which I shal with dissymulyng amende.
And beth nat wroth, I have ek understonde
How ye ne do but holden me in honde.   1615
But now no force, I kan nat in yow gesse
But alle trouthe and alle gentilesse.

79

'Come I wole; but yet in swich disjoynte
I stonde as now, that what yer or what day
That this shal be, that kan I naught apoynte.   1620
But in effect I pray yow, as I may,
Of youre good word and of youre frendship ay.
For trewely, while that my lif may dure,
As for a frend ye may in me assure.

'Yet preye ich yow, on yvel ye ne take   1625
That it is short which that I to yow write;
I dar nat, ther I am, wel lettres make,
Ne nevere yet ne koude I wel endite.
Ek gret effect men write in place lite;
Th'entente is al, and nat the lettres space.   1630
And fareth now wel, God have yow in his grace!
                    La vostre C.'   1631

Book V Envoy

Go, litel bok, go, litel myn tragedye,   1786
Ther God thi makere yet, er that he dye,
So sende myght to make in som comedye!
But litel book, no makyng thow n'envie,
But subgit be to alle poesye;   1790
And kis the steppes, where as thow seest pace
Virgile, Ovide, Omer, Lucan, and Stace.

And for ther is so gret diversite
In Englissh and in writyng of oure tonge,
So prey I God that non myswrite the,   1795
Ne the mysmetre for defaute of tonge.
And red wherso thow be, or elles songe,
That thow be understonde, God I biseche!
But yet to purpos of my rather speche.—

The wrath, as I bigan yow for to seye,   1800
Of Troilus the Grekis boughten deere.
For thousandes his hondes maden deye,
As he that was withouten any peere,
Save Ector, in his tyme, as I kan heere.
But weilawey, save only Goddes wille!   1805
Despitously hym slough the fierse Achille.

And whan that he was slayn in this manere,
His lighte goost ful blisfully is went
Up to the holughnesse of the eighthe spere,
In convers letyng everich element;   1810
And ther he saugh, with ful avysement,
The erratik sterres, herkenyng armonye
With sownes ful of hevenyssh melodie.

And down from thennes faste he gan avyse
This litel spot of erthe, that with the se   1815
Embraced is, and fully gan despise
This wrecched world, and held al vanite
To respect of the pleyn felicite
That is in hevene above; and at the laste,
Ther he was slayn, his lokyng down he caste.   1820

And in hymself he lough right at the wo
Of hem that wepten for his deth so faste;
And dampned al oure werk that foloweth so
The blynde lust, the which that may nat laste,
And sholden al oure herte on heven caste.   1825
And forth he wente, shortly for to telle,
Ther as Mercurye sorted hym to dwelle.

Swich fyn hath, lo, this Troilus for love!
Swich fyn hath al his grete worthynesse!
Swich fyn hath his estat real above,   1830

Swich fyn his lust, swich fyn hath his noblesse!
Swych fyn hath false worldes brotelnesse!
And thus bigan his lovyng of Criseyde,
As I have told, and in this wise he deyde.

O yonge, fresshe folkes, he or she,   183
In which that love up groweth with youre age,
Repeyreth hom fro worldly vanyte,
And of youre herte up casteth the visage
To thilke God that after his ymage
Yow made, and thynketh al nys but a faire   184
This world, that passeth soone as floures faire.

And loveth hym, the which that right for love
Upon a crois, oure soules for to beye,
First starf, and roos, and sit in hevene above;
For he nyl falsen no wight, dar I seye,   184
That wol his herte al holly on hym leye.
And syn he best to love is, and most meke,
What nedeth feynede loves for to seke?

Lo here, of payens corsed olde rites,
Lo here, what alle hire goddes may availle;   185
Lo here, thise wrecched worldes appetites;
Lo here, the fyn and guerdoun for travaille
Of Jove, Appollo, of Mars, of swich rascaille!
Lo here, the forme of olde clerkis speche
In poetrie, if ye hire bokes seche.   185

O moral Gower, this book I directe
To the and to the, philosophical Strode,
To vouchen sauf, ther nede is, to correcte,
Of youre benignites and zeles goode.
And to that sothefast Crist, that starf on rode,   186

With al myn herte of mercy evere I preye,
And to the Lord right thus I speke and seye:

Thow oon, and two, and thre, eterne on lyve,
That regnest ay in thre, and two, and oon,
Uncircumscript, and al maist circumscrive,   1865
Us from visible and invisible foon
Defende, and to thy mercy, everichon,
So make us, Jesus, for thi mercy digne,
For love of mayde and moder thyn benigne.   1869
      Amen.

The Legend of Good Women

from *The Prologue*

A thousand tymes have I herd men telle
That ther ys joy in hevene and peyne in helle,
And I acorde wel that it ys so;
But, natheles, yet wot I wel also
That ther nis noon dwellyng in this contree,   5
That eyther hath in hevene or helle ybe
Ne may of hit noon other weyes witen,
But as he hath herd seyd, or founde it writen;
For by assay ther may no man it preve.
But God forbede but men shulde leve   10
Wel more thing then men han seen with ye!
Men shal not wenen every thing a lye
But yf himself yt seeth, or elles dooth;
For, God wot, thing is never the lasse sooth,

Thogh every wight ne may it nat ysee.   15
Bernard the monk ne saugh nat all, pardee!
    Than mote we to bokes that we fynde,
Thurgh whiche that olde thinges ben in mynde,
And to the doctrine of these olde wyse,
Yeve credence, in every skylful wise,   20
That tellen of these olde appreved stories
Of holynesse, of regnes, of victories,
Of love, of hate, of other sondry thynges,
Of whiche I may not maken rehersynges.
And yf that olde bokes were aweye,   25
Yloren were of remembraunce the keye.
Wel ought us thanne honouren and beleve
These bokes, there we han noon other preve.
    And as for me, though that I konne but lyte,
On bokes for to rede I me delyte,   30
And to hem yive I feyth and ful credence,
And in myn herte have hem in reverence
So hertely, that ther is game noon
That fro my bokes maketh me to goon,
But yt be seldom on the holyday,   35
Save, certeynly, whan that the month of May
Is comen, and that I here the foules synge,
And that the floures gynnen for to sprynge,
Farewel my bok, and my devocioun!
    Now have I thanne eek this condicioun,   40
That, of al the floures in the mede,
Thanne love I most thise floures white and rede,
Swiche as men callen daysyes in our toun.
To hem have I so gret affeccioun,
As I seyde erst, whanne comen is the May,   45
That in my bed ther daweth me no day
That I nam up and walkyng in the mede
To seen this flour ayein the sonne sprede,
Whan it upryseth erly by the morwe.

That blisful sighte softneth al my sorwe,   50
So glad am I, whan that I have presence
Of it, to doon it alle reverence,
As she that is of alle floures flour,
Fulfilled of al vertu and honour,
And evere ilyke faire, and fressh of hewe;   55
And I love it, and ever ylike newe,
And evere shal, til that myn herte dye.
Al swere I nat, of this I wol nat lye;
Ther loved no wight hotter in his lyve.
And whan that hit ys eve, I renne blyve,   60
As sone as evere the sonne gynneth weste,
To seen this flour, how it wol go to reste,
For fere of nyght, so hateth she derknesse.
Hire chere is pleynly sprad in the brightnesse
Of the sonne, for ther yt wol unclose.   65
Allas, that I ne had Englyssh, ryme or prose,
Suffisant this flour to preyse aryght!
But helpeth, ye that han konnyng and myght,
Ye lovers that kan make of sentement;
In this cas oghte ye be diligent   70
To forthren me somwhat in my labour,
Whethir ye ben with the leef or with the flour.
For wel I wot that ye han her-biforn
Of makyng ropen, and lad awey the corn,
And I come after, glenyng here and there,   75
And am ful glad yf I may fynde an ere
Of any goodly word that ye han left.
And thogh it happen me rehercen eft
That ye han in your fresshe songes sayd,
Forbereth me, and beth nat evele apayd,   80
Syn that ye see I do yt in the honour
Of love, and eke in service of the flour
Whom that I serve as I have wit or myght.
She is the clernesse and the verray lyght

That in this derke world me wynt and ledeth.   85
The hert in-with my sorwfull brest yow dredeth
And loveth so sore that ye ben verrayly
The maistresse of my wit, and nothing I.
My word, my werk ys knyt so in youre bond
That, as an harpe obeieth to the hond   90
And maketh it soune after his fyngerynge,
Ryght so mowe ye oute of myn herte bringe
Swich vois, ryght as yow lyst, to laughe or pleyne.
Be ye my gide and lady sovereyne!
As to myn erthly god to yow I calle,   95
Bothe in this werk and in my sorwes alle.
    But wherfore that I spak, to yive credence
To olde stories and doon hem reverence,
And that men mosten more thyng beleve
Then men may seen at eye, or elles preve,—   100
That shal I seyn, whanne that I see my tyme;
I may not al at-ones speke in ryme.
My besy gost, that thursteth alwey newe
To seen this flour so yong, so fressh of hewe,
Constreyned me with so gledy desir   105
That in myn herte I feele yet the fir
That made me to ryse, er yt were day—
And this was now the firste morwe of May—
With dredful hert and glad devocioun,
For to ben at the resureccioun   110
Of this flour, whan that yt shulde unclose
Agayn the sonne, that roos as red as rose,
That in the brest was of the beste, that day,
That Agenores doghtre ladde away.
And doun on knes anoon-ryght I me sette,   115
And, as I koude, this fresshe flour I grette,
Knelyng alwey, til it unclosed was,
Upon the smale, softe, swote gras,
That was with floures swote enbrouded al,

Of swich swetnesse and swich odour overal,   120
That, for to speke of gomme, or herbe, or tree,
Comparisoun may noon ymaked bee;
For yt surmounteth pleynly alle odoures,
And of riche beaute alle floures.
Forgeten hadde the erthe his pore estat   125
Of wynter, that hym naked made and mat,
And with his swerd of cold so sore greved;
Now hath th'atempre sonne all that releved,
That naked was, and clad him new agayn.
The smale foules, of the sesoun fayn,   130
That from the panter and the net ben scaped,
Upon the foweler, that hem made awhaped
In wynter, and distroyed hadde hire brood,
In his dispit hem thoghte yt did hem good
To synge of hym, and in hir song despise   135
The foule cherl that, for his coveytise,
Had hem betrayed with his sophistrye.
This was hire song, 'The foweler we deffye,
And al his craft.' And somme songen clere
Layes of love, that joye it was to here,   140
In worship and in preysinge of hir make;
And for the newe blisful somers sake,
Upon the braunches ful of blosmes softe,
In hire delyt they turned hem ful ofte,
And songen, 'Blessed be Seynt Valentyn,   145
For on this day I chees yow to be myn,
Withouten repentyng, myn herte swete!'
And therwithalle hire bekes gonnen meete,
Yeldyng honour and humble obeysaunces
To love, and diden hire other observaunces   150
That longeth onto love and to nature;
Construeth that as yow lyst, I do no cure.
And thoo that hadde doon unkyndenesse—
As dooth the tydif, for newfangelnesse—

Besoghte mercy of hir trespassynge,   155
And humblely songen hire repentynge,
And sworen on the blosmes to be trewe,
So that hire makes wolde upon hem rewe,
And at the laste maden hire acord.
Al founde they Daunger for a tyme a lord,   160
Yet Pitee, thurgh his stronge gentil myght,
Forgaf, and made Mercy passen Ryght,
Thurgh innocence and ruled Curtesye.
But I ne clepe nat innocence folye,
Ne fals pitee, for vertu is the mene,   165
As Etik seith; in swich maner I mene.
And thus thise foweles, voide of al malice,
Acordeden to love, and laften vice
Of hate, and songen alle of oon acord,
'Welcome, somer, oure governour and lord!'   170
   And Zepherus and Flora gentilly
Yaf to the floures, softe and tenderly,
Hire swoote breth, and made hem for to sprede.
As god and goddesse of the floury mede;
In which me thoghte I myghte, day by day,   175
Dwellen alwey, the joly month of May,
Withouten slep, withouten mete or drynke.
Adoun ful softely I gan to synke,
And lenynge on myn elbowe and my syde,
The longe day I shoop me for t'abide   180
For nothing elles, and I shal nat lye,
But for to loke upon the dayesie,
That wel by reson men it calle may
The 'dayesye' or elles the 'ye of day,'
The emperice and flour of floures all.   185
I pray to God that faire mote she falle,
And alle that loven floures, for hire sake!
But natheles, ne wene nat that I make
In preysing of the flour agayn the leef,

No more than of the corn agayn the sheef;   190
For, as to me, nys lever noon ne lother.
I nam withholden yit with never nother;
Ne I not who serveth leef, ne who the flour.
Wel browken they her service or labour;
For this thing is al of another tonne,   195
Of olde storye, er swich stryf was begonne.
    Whan that the sonne out of the south gan weste,
And that this flour gan close and goon to reste
For derknesse of the nyght, the which she dredde,
Hom to myn hous ful swiftly I me spedde   200
To goon to reste, and erly for to ryse,
To seen this flour to sprede, as I devyse.
And in a litel herber that I have,
That benched was on turves fressh ygrave,
I bad men sholde me my couche make;   205
For deyntee of the newe someres sake,
I bad hem strawen floures on my bed.
Whan I was leyd, and had myn eyen hed,
I fel on slepe within an houre or twoo.
Me mette how I lay in the medewe thoo,   210
To seen this flour that I so love and drede;
And from afer com walkyng in the mede
The god of Love, and in his hand a quene,
And she was clad in real habit grene.
A fret of gold she hadde next her heer,   215
And upon that a whit corowne she beer
With flourouns smale, and I shal nat lye;
For al the world, ryght as a dayesye
Ycorouned ys with white leves lyte,
So were the flowrouns of hire coroune white.   220
For of o perle fyn, oriental,
Hire white coroune was ymaked al;
For which the white coroune above the grene
Made hire lyk a daysie for to sene,

Considered eke hir fret of gold above. 225
   Yclothed was this myghty god of Love
In silk, enbrouded ful of grene greves,
In-with a fret of rede rose-leves,
The fresshest syn the world was first bygonne.
His gilte heer was corowned with a sonne, 230
Instede of gold, for hevynesse and wyghte.
Therwith me thoghte his face shoon so bryghte
That wel unnethes myghte I him beholde;
And in his hand me thoghte I saugh him holde
Twoo firy dartes, as the gledes rede, 235
And aungelyke hys wynges saugh I sprede.
And al be that men seyn that blynd ys he,
Algate me thoghte that he myghte se;
For sternely on me he gan byholde,
So that his loking dooth myn herte colde. 240
And by the hand he held this noble quene,
Corowned with whit, and clothed al in grene,
So womanly, so benigne, and so meke,
That in this world, thogh that men wolde seke,
Half hire beaute shulde men nat fynde 245
In creature that formed ys by kynde.
And therfore may I seyn, as thynketh me,
This song in preysyng of this lady fre.

Balade

   Hyd, Absolon, thy gilte tresses clere;
Ester, ley thou thy meknesse al adown; 250
Hyd, Jonathas, al thy frendly manere;
Penalopee and Marcia Catoun,
Make of youre wifhod no comparysoun;
Hyde ye youre beautes, Ysoude and Eleyne:
My lady cometh, that al this may disteyne. 255

Thy faire body, lat yt nat appere,
Lavyne; and thou, Lucresse of Rome toun,
And Polixene, that boghten love so dere,
And Cleopatre, with al thy passyoun,
Hyde ye your trouthe of love and your renoun;   260
And thou, Tisbe, that hast for love swich peyne:
My lady cometh, that al this may disteyne.

Herro, Dido, Laudomia, alle yfere,
And Phillis, hangyng for thy Demophoun,
And Canace, espied by thy chere,   265
Ysiphile, betrayed with Jasoun,
Maketh of your trouthe neythir boost ne soun;
Nor Ypermystre or Adriane, ye tweyne:
My lady cometh, that al this may dysteyne.   269

The Legend of Cleopatra

After the deth of Tholome the kyng,   580
That al Egipt hadde in his governyng,
Regned his queene Cleopataras;
Tyl on a tyme befel there swich a cas,
That out of Rome was sent a senatour,
For to conqueren regnes and honour   585
Unto the toun of Rome, as was usaunce,
To han the world at hire obeÿsaunce,
And soth to seyne, Antonius was his name.
So fil it, as Fortune hym oughte a shame,
Whan he was fallen in prosperite,   590
Rebel unto the toun of Rome is he.
And over al this, the suster of Cesar,
He lafte hire falsly, or that she was war,
And wolde algates han another wyf;
For which he tok with Rome and Cesar stryf.   595

Natheles, for sothe, this ilke senatour
Was a ful worthy gentil werreyour,
And of his deth it was ful gret damage.
But love hadde brought this man in swich a rage,
And hym so narwe bounden in his las,   60
Al for the love of Cleopataras,
That al the world he sette at no value.
Hym thoughte there nas nothyng to hym so due
As for Cleopataras for to love and serve;
Hym roughte nat in armes for to sterve   60
In the defence of hyre and of hire ryght.
This noble queene ek lovede so this knyght,
Thourgh his desert, and for his chyvalrye;
As certeynly, but if that bokes lye,
He was, of persone and of gentillesse,   61
And of discrecioun and hardynesse,
Worthi to any wyght that liven may;
And she was fayr as is the rose in May.
And, for to make shortly is the beste,
She wax his wif, and hadde hym as hire leste.   61
    The weddynge and the feste to devyse,
To me, that have ytake swich empryse
Of so many a story for to make,
It were to longe, lest that I shulde slake
Of thyng that bereth more effect and charge;   62
For men may overlade a ship or barge.
And forthy to th'effect thanne wol I skyppe,
And al the remenaunt, I wol lete it slippe.
    Octovyan, that wod was of this dede,
Shop hym an ost on Antony to lede   62
Al uterly for his destruccioun.
With stoute Romeyns, crewel as lyoun,
To ship they wente, and thus I lat hem sayle.
Antonius was war, and wol nat fayle
To meten with these Romeyns, if he may;   63

Tok ek his red, and bothe, upon a day,
His wif and he, and al his ost, forth wente
To shipe anon, no lengere they ne stente;
And in the se it happede hem to mete.
Up goth the trompe, and for to shoute and shete,   635
And peynen hem to sette on with the sunne.
With grysely soun out goth the grete gonne,
And heterly they hurtelen al atones,
And from the top doun come the grete stones.
In goth the grapenel, so ful of crokes;   640
Among the ropes renne the sherynge-hokes.
In with the polax preseth he and he;
Byhynde the mast begynnyth he to fle,
And out ageyn, and dryveth hym overbord;
He styngeth hym upon his speres ord;   645
He rent the seyl with hokes lyke a sithe;
He bryngeth the cuppe, and biddeth hem be blythe;
He poureth pesen upon the haches slidere;
With pottes ful of lyme they gon togidere;
And thus the longe day in fyght they spende,   650
Tyl at the laste, as every thyng hath ende,
Antony is schent, and put hym to the flyghte,
And al his folk to-go, that best go myghte.
    Fleth ek the queen, with al hire purpre sayl,
For strokes, whiche that wente as thikke as hayl;   655
No wonder was she myghte it nat endure.
And whan that Antony saw that aventure,
'Allas,' quod he, 'the day that I was born!
My worshipe in this day thus have I lorn.'
And for dispeyr out of his wit he sterte,   660
And rof hymself anon thourghout the herte,
Or that he ferther wente out of the place.
His wif, that coude of Cesar have no grace,
To Egipt is fled for drede and for destresse.
But herkeneth, ye that speken of kyndenesse,   665

Ye men that falsly sweren many an oth
That ye wol deye, if that youre love be wroth,
Here may ye sen of wemen which a trouthe!
This woful Cleopatre hath mad swich routhe
That there is tonge non that may it telle.   670
But on the morwe she wolde no lengere dwelle,
But made hire subtyl werkmen make a shryne
Of alle the rubyes and the stones fyne
In al Egypte, that she coude espie,
And putte ful the shryne of spicerye,   675
And let the cors enbaume, and forth she fette
This dede cors, and in the shryne it shette.
And next the shryne a pit thanne doth she grave,
And alle the serpentes that she myghte have,
She putte hem in that grave, and thus she seyde: 680
'Now, love, to whom my sorweful herte obeyde
So ferforthly that from that blisful houre
That I yow swor to ben al frely youre—
I mene yow, Antonius, my knyght—
That nevere wakynge, in the day or nyght,   685
Ye nere out of myn hertes remembraunce,
For wel or wo, for carole or for daunce;
And in myself this covenaunt made I tho,
That ryght swich as ye felten, wel or wo,
As fer forth as it in my power lay,   690
Unreprovable unto my wyfhod ay,
The same wolde I fele, lyf or deth,—
And thilke covenant, whil me lasteth breth,
I wol fulfille; and that shal ben wel sene,
Was nevere unto hire love a trewer quene.'   695
And with that word, naked, with ful good herte,
Among the serpents in the pit she sterte,
And there she ches to have hire buryinge.
Anon the nadderes gonne hire for to stynge,
And she hire deth receyveth with good cheere,   700

For love of Antony that was hire so dere.
And this is storyal soth, it is no fable.
Now, or I fynde a man thus trewe and stable,
And wol for love his deth so frely take,
I preye God let oure hedes nevere ake! Amen.   705

The Complaint unto Pity

Pite, that I have sought so yore agoo,
With herte soore, and ful of besy peyne,
That in this world was never wight so woo
Withoute deth,—and, yf I shal not feyne,
My purpos was to Pite to compleyne   5
Upon the crueltee and tirannye
Of Love, that for my trouthe doth me dye.

And when that I, be lengthe of certeyne yeres,
Had evere in oon a tyme sought to speke,
To Pitee ran I, al bespreynt with teres,   10
To prayen hir on Cruelte me awreke.
But er I myghte with any word outbreke,
Or tellen any of my peynes smerte,
I fond hir ded, and buried in an herte.

Adoun I fel when that I saugh the herse,   15
Ded as a ston, while that the swogh me laste;
But up I roos, with colour ful dyverse,
And pitously on hir myn eyen I caste,
And ner the corps I gan to presen faste,

And for the soule I shop me for to preye.   20
I nas but lorn; ther was no more to seye.

Thus am I slayn, sith that Pite is ded.
Allas, that day! that ever hyt shulde falle!
What maner man dar now hold up his hed?
To whom shal any sorwful herte calle?   25
Now Cruelte hath cast to slee us alle,
In ydel hope, folk redeless of peyne,—
Syth she is ded, to whom shul we compleyne?

But yet encreseth me this wonder newe,
That no wight woot that she is ded, but I—   30
So many men as in her tyme hir knewe—
And yet she dyed not so sodeynly;
For I have sought hir ever ful besely
Sith first I hadde wit or mannes mynde;
But she was ded er that I koude hir fynde.   35

Aboute hir herse there stoden lustely,
Withouten any woo, as thoughte me,
Bounte parfyt, wel armed and richely,
And fresshe Beaute, Lust, and Jolyte,
Assured Maner, Youthe, and Honeste,   40
Wisdom, Estaat, Drede, and Governaunce,
Confedred both by bonde and alliaunce.

A compleynt had I, writen, in myn hond,
For to have put to Pittee as a bille;
But when I al this companye ther fond,   45
That rather wolden al my cause spille
Then do me help, I held my pleynte stille;
For to that folk, withouten any fayle,
Withoute Pitee ther may no bille availe.

Then leve I al these vertues, sauf Pite, 50
Kepynge the corps, as ye have herd me seyn,
Confedered all by bond of Cruelte,
And ben assented when I shal be sleyn.
And I have put my complaynt up ageyn;
For to my foes my bille I dar not shewe, 55
Th'effect of which seith thus, in wordes fewe:—

The Bill of Complaint

Humblest of herte, highest of reverence,
Benygne flour, coroune of vertues alle,
Sheweth unto youre rial excellence
Youre servaunt, yf I durste me so calle, 60
Hys mortal harm, in which he is yfalle;
And noght al oonly for his evel fare,
But for your renoun, as he shal declare.

Hit stondeth thus: your contraire, Crueltee,
Allyed is ayenst your regalye, 65
Under colour of womanly Beaute,—
For men shulde not, lo, knowe hir tirannye,—
With Bounte, Gentilesse, and Curtesye,
And hath depryved yow now of your place
That hyghte 'Beaute apertenant to Grace.' 70

For kyndely, by youre herytage ryght,
Ye ben annexed ever unto Bounte;
And verrayly ye oughte do youre myght
To helpe Trouthe in his adversyte.
Ye be also the corowne of Beaute; 75
And certes, yf ye wanten in these tweyne,
The world is lore; ther is no more to seyne.

Eke what availeth Maner and Gentilesse
Withoute yow, benygne creature?
Shal Cruelte be your governeresse?   8o
Allas! what herte may hyt longe endure?
Wherfore, but ye the rather take cure
To breke that perilouse alliaunce,
Ye sleen hem that ben in your obeisaunce.

And further over, yf ye suffre this,   85
Youre renoun ys fordoo than in a throwe;
Ther shal no man wite well what Pite is.
Allas, that your renoun sholde be so lowe!
Ye be than fro youre heritage ythrowe
By Cruelte, that occupieth youre place;   9o
And we despeyred, that seken to your grace.

Have mercy on me, thow Herenus quene,
That yow have sought so tendirly and yore;
Let som strem of youre lyght on me be sene
That love and drede yow, ever lenger the more.   9.
For, sothly for to seyne, I bere the soore;
And, though I be not konnynge for to pleyne,
For Goddis love, have mercy on my peyne!

My peyne is this, that what so I desire
That have I not, ne nothing lyk therto;   100
And ever setteth Desir myn hert on fire.
Eke on that other syde, where so I goo,
What maner thing that may encrese my woo,
That have I redy, unsoght, everywhere;
Me [ne] lakketh but my deth, and than my bere.   10.

What nedeth to shewe parcel of my peyne?
Syth every woo that herte may bethynke
I suffre, and yet I dar not to yow pleyne;

For wel I wot, although I wake or wynke,
Ye rekke not whether I flete or synke.   110
But natheles, yet my trouthe I shal sustene
Unto my deth, and that shal wel be sene.

This is to seyne, I wol be youres evere;
Though ye me slee by Crueltee, your foo,
Algate my spirit shal never dissevere   115
Fro your servise, for any peyne or woo.
Sith ye be ded—allas, that hyt is soo!—
Thus for your deth I may wel wepe and pleyne
With herte sore, and ful of besy peyne.

To Rosemounde

A Balade

MADAME, ye ben of al beaute shryne
As fer as cercled is the mapemounde,
For as the cristal glorious ye shyne,
And lyke ruby ben your chekes rounde.
Therwith ye ben so mery and so jocounde   5
That at a revel whan that I see you daunce,
It is an oynement unto my wounde,
Thogh ye to me ne do no daliaunce.

For thogh I wepe of teres ful a tyne,
Yet may that wo myn herte nat confounde;   10
Your semy voys, that ye so smal out twyne,
Maketh my thoght in joy and blis habounde.
So curtaysly I go, with love bounde,

That to myself I sey, in my penaunce,
'Suffyseth me to love you, Rosemounde,   15
Thogh ye to me ne do no daliaunce.'

Nas never pyk walwed in galauntyne
As I in love am walwed and ywounde,
For which ful ofte I of myself devyne
That I am trewe Tristam the secounde.   20
My love may not refreyde nor affounde;
I brenne ay in an amorous plesaunce.
Do what you lyst, I wyl your thral be founde,
Thogh ye to me ne do no daliaunce.

Womanly Noblesse

Balade That Chaucier Made

So hath myn herte caught in remembraunce
Your beaute hoole and stidefast governaunce,
Your vertues alle and your hie noblesse,
That you to serve is set al my plesaunce.
So wel me liketh your womanly contenaunce,   5
Your fresshe fetures and your comlynesse,
That whiles I live, myn herte to his maystresse
You hath ful chose in trewe perséveraunce
Never to chaunge, for no maner distresse.

And sith I shal do [you] this observaunce   10
Al my lif, withouten displesaunce,
You for to serve with al my besynesse,

. . . .

And have me somwhat in your souvenaunce.
My woful herte suffreth greet duresse;
And [loke how humblely], with al symplesse,   15
My wyl I cónforme to your ordynaunce
As you best list, my peynes for to redresse.

Considryng eke how I hange in balaunce,
In your service, such, lo! is my chaunce,
Abidyng grace, whan that your gentilnesse,   20
Of my grete wo listeth don alleggeaunce,
And wyth your pite me som wise avaunce,
In ful rebatyng of myn hevynesse,
And thynketh by resoun that wommanly noblesse
Shulde nat desire for to do the outrance   25
Ther as she fyndeth non unbuxumnesse.

Lenvoye

Auctour of norture, lady of plesaunce,
Soveraigne of beautee, flour of wommanhede,
Take ye non hede unto myn ignoraunce,
But this receyveth of your goodlihede,   30
Thynkyng that I have caught in remembraunce,
Your beaute hole, your stidefast governaunce.

Chaucers Wordes unto Adam, His Owne Scriveyn

ADAM scriveyn, if ever it thee bifalle
Boece or Troylus for to wryten newe,
Under thy long lokkes thou most have the scalle,

But after my makyng thou wryte more trewe;
So ofte a-daye I mot thy werk renewe,   5
It to correcte and eek to rubbe and scrape;
And al is thorugh thy negligence and rape.

The Former Age

A BLISFUL lyf, a paisible and a swete,
Ledden the peples in the former age.
They helde hem payed of the fruites that they ete,
Which that the feldes yave hem by usage;
They ne were nat forpampred with outrage.   5
Unknowen was the quern and eek the melle;
They eten mast, hawes, and swich pounage,
And dronken water of the colde welle.

Yit nas the ground nat wounded with the plough,
But corn up-sprong, unsowe of mannes hond,   10
The which they gnodded, and eete nat half ynough.
No man yit knew the forwes of his lond;
No man the fyr out of the flint yit fond;
Unkorven and ungrobbed lay the vyne;
No man yit in the morter spyces grond   15
To clarre, ne to sause of galantyne.

No mader, welde, or wood no litestere
Ne knew; the flees was of his former hewe;
No flesh ne wiste offence of egge or spere;
No coyn ne knew man which was fals or trewe;   20
No ship yit karf the wawes grene and blewe;

No marchaunt yit ne fette outlandish ware;
No trompes for the werres folk ne knewe,
Ne toures heye and walles rounde or square.

What sholde it han avayled to werreye?   25
Ther lay no profit, ther was no richesse,
But cursed was the tyme, I dare wel seye,
That men first dide hir swety bysinesse
To grobbe up metal, lurkinge in derknesse,
And in the riveres first gemmes soghte.   30
Allas! than sprong up al the cursednesse
Of coveytyse, that first our sorwe broghte!

Thise tyraunts putte hem gladly nat in pres
No wildnesse ne no busshes for to winne;
Ther poverte is, as seith Diogenes,   35
Ther as vitaile is eek so skars and thinne
That noght but mast or apples is therinne.
But, ther as bagges been and fat vitaile,
Ther wol they gon, and spare for no sinne
With al hir ost the cite for t'assaile.   40

Yit were no paleis-chaumbres, ne non halles;
In caves and [in] wodes softe and swete
Slepten this blissed folk withoute walles,
On gras or leves in parfit quiete.
Ne doun of fetheres, ne no bleched shete   45
Was kid to hem, but in seurtee they slepte.
Hir hertes were al oon, withoute galles;
Everich of hem his feith to other kepte.

Unforged was the hauberk and the plate;
The lambish peple, voyd of alle vyce,   50
Hadden no fantasye to debate,
But ech of hem wolde other wel cheryce;

No pryde, non envye, non avaryce,
No lord, no taylage by no tyrannye;
Humblesse and pees, good feith, the emperice,   55

    .   .   .   .   .   .

Yit was not Jupiter the likerous,
That first was fader of delicacye,
Come in this world; ne Nembrot, desirous
To regne, had nat maad his toures hye.
Allas, allas! now may men wepe and crye!   60
For in oure dayes nis but covetyse,
Doublenesse, and tresoun, and envye,
Poyson, manslauhtre, and mordre in sondry wyse.

Fortune

Balades de Visage sanz Peinture

I. Le Pleintif countre Fortune

THIS wrecched worldes transmutacioun,
As wele or wo, now povre and now honour,
Withouten ordre or wys discrecioun
Governed is by Fortunes errour.
But natheles, the lak of hir favour   5
Ne may nat don me singen, though I dye,
'Jay tout perdu mon temps et mon labour;'
For fynally, Fortune, I thee defye!

Yit is me left the light of my resoun,
To knowen frend fro fo in thy mirour.   10
So muchel hath yit thy whirling up and doun

Ytaught me for to knowen in an hour.
But trewely, no force of thy reddour
To him that over himself hath the maystrye!
My suffisaunce shal be my socour;   15
For fynally, Fortune, I thee defye!

O Socrates, thou stidfast champioun,
She never mighte be thy tormentour;
Thou never dreddest hir oppressioun,
Ne in hir chere founde thou no savour.   20
Thou knewe wel the deceit of hir colour,
And that hir moste worshipe is to lye.
I knowe hir eek a fals dissimulour;
For fynally, Fortune, I thee defye!

II. *La respounse de Fortune au Pleintif*

No man is wrecched, but himself it wene,   25
And he that hath himself hath suffisaunce.
Why seystow thanne I am to thee so kene,
That hast thyself out of my governaunce?
Sey thus: 'Graunt mercy of thyn haboundaunce
That thou hast lent or this.' Why wolt thou stryve?   30
What wostow yit how I thee wol avaunce?
And eek thou hast thy beste frend alyve.

I have thee taught divisioun bitwene
Frend of effect, and frend of countenaunce;
Thee nedeth nat the galle of noon hyene,   35
That cureth eyen derked for penaunce;
Now seestow cleer, that were in ignoraunce.
Yit halt thyn ancre, and yit thou mayst arryve
Ther bountee berth the keye of my substaunce;
And eek thou hast thy beste frend alyve.   40

How many have I refused to sustene,
Sin I thee fostred have in thy plesaunce!
Woltow than make a statut on thy quene
That I shal been ay at thyn ordinaunce?
Thou born art in my regne of variaunce,   45
Aboute the wheel with other most thou dryve.
My lore is bet than wikke is thy grevaunce;
And eek thou hast thy beste frend alyve.

III. La respounse du Pleintif countre Fortune

Thy lore I dampne, it is adversitee.
My frend maystow nat reven, blind goddesse   50
That I thy frendes knowe, I thanke hit thee.
Tak hem agayn, lat hem go lye on presse!
The negardye in keping hir richesse
Prenostik is thou wolt hir tour assayle;
Wikke appetyt comth ay before syknesse: 55
In general, this reule may nat fayle.

La respounse de Fortune countre le Pleintif

Thou pinchest at my mutabilitee,
For I thee lente a drope of my richesse,
And now me lyketh to withdrawe me.
Why sholdestow my realtee oppresse?   60
The see may ebbe and flowen more or lesse;
The welkne hath might to shyne, reyne, or hayle;
Right so mot I kythen my brotelnesse:
In general, this reule may nat fayle.

Lo, th'execucion of the majestee   65
That al purveyeth of his rightwysnesse,

That same thing 'Fortune' clepen ye,
Ye blinde bestes, ful of lewednesse!
The hevene hath propretee of sikernesse,
This world hath ever resteles travayle;   70
The laste day is ende of myn intresse:
In general, this reule may nat fayle.

Princes, I prey you, of your gentilesse,
Lat nat this man on me thus crye and pleyne,
And I shal quyte you your bisinesse   75
At my requeste, as three of you or tweyne;
And, but you list releve him of his peyne,
Preyeth his beste frend, of his noblesse,
That to som beter estat he may atteyne.

Truth

Balade de Bon Conseyl

FLEE fro the prees, and dwelle with sothfastnesse,
Suffyce unto thy good, though it be smal;
For hord hath hate, and climbing tikelnesse,
Prees hath envye, and wele blent overal;
Savour no more than thee bihove shal;   5
Reule wel thyself, that other folk canst rede;
And trouthe thee shal delivere, it is no drede.

Tempest thee noght al croked to redresse,
In trust of hir that turneth as a bal:

Gret reste stant in litel besinesse;

Be war also to sporne ayeyns an al;

Stryve not, as doth the crokke with the wal.

Daunte thyself, that dauntest otheres dede;

And trouthe thee shal delivere, it is no drede.

That thee is sent, receyve in buxumnesse;

The wrastling for this world axeth a fal.

Her is non hoom, her nis but wildernesse:

Forth, pilgrim, forth! Forth, beste, out of thy stal!

Know thy contree, look up, thank God of al;

Hold the heye wey, and lat thy gost thee lede;

And trouthe thee shal delivere, it is no drede.

Envoy

Therfore, thou Vache, leve thyn old wrecchednesse;

Unto the world leve now to be thral;

Crye him mercy, that of his hy goodnesse

Made thee of noght, and in especial

Draw unto him, and pray in general

For thee, and eek for other, hevenlich mede;

And trouthe thee shal delivere, it is no drede.

Gentilesse

Moral Balade of Chaucier

THE firste stok, fader of gentilesse—

What man that claymeth gentil for to be

Must folowe his trace, and alle his wittes dresse
Vertu to sewe, and vyces for to flee.
For unto vertu longeth dignitee,   5
And noght the revers, saufly dar I deme,
Al were he mytre, croune, or diademe.

This firste stok was ful of rightwisnesse,
Trewe of his word, sobre, pitous, and free,
Clene of his gost, and loved besinesse,   10
Ayeinst the vyce of slouthe, in honestee;
And, by his heir love vertu, as dide he,
He is noght gentil, thogh he riche seme,
Al were he mytre, croune, or diademe.

Vyce may wel be heir to old richesse;   15
But ther may no man, as men may wel see,
Bequethe his heir his vertuous noblesse
(That is appropred unto no degree
But to the firste fader in magestee,
That maketh hem his heyres that him queme),   20
Al were he mytre, croune, or diademe.

Lak of Stedfastnesse

Balade

SOMTYME the world was so stedfast and stable
That mannes word was obligacioun;
And now it is so fals and deceivable
That word and deed, as in conclusioun,
Ben nothing lyk, for turned up-so-doun   5

Is al this world for mede and wilfulnesse,
That al is lost for lak of stedfastnesse.

What maketh this world to be so variable
But lust that folk have in dissensioun?
For among us now a man is holde unable,   10
But if he can, by som collusioun,
Don his neighbour wrong or oppressioun.
What causeth this but wilful wrecchednesse,
That al is lost for lak of stedfastnesse?

Trouthe is put doun, resoun is holden fable;   15
Vertu hath now no dominacioun;
Pitee exyled, no man is merciable;
Through covetyse is blent discrecioun.
The world hath mad a permutacioun
Fro right to wrong, fro trouthe to fikelnesse,   20
That al is lost for lak of stedfastnesse.

Lenvoy to King Richard

O prince, desyre to be honourable,
Cherish thy folk and hate extorcioun!
Suffre nothing that may be reprevable
To thyn estat don in thy regioun.   25
Shew forth thy swerd of castigacioun,
Dred God, do law, love trouthe and worthinesse,
And wed thy folk agein to stedfastnesse.

The Complaint of Venus

THER nys so high comfort to my pleasaunce,
When that I am in any hevynesse,
As for to have leyser of remembraunce
Upon the manhod and the worthynesse,
Upon the trouthe and on the stidfastnesse   5
Of him whos I am al, while I may dure.
Ther oghte blame me no creature,
For every wight preiseth his gentilesse.

In him is bounte, wysdom, governaunce,
Wel more then any mannes wit can gesse;   10
For grace hath wold so ferforth hym avaunce
That of knyghthod he is parfit richesse.
Honour honoureth him for his noblesse;
Therto so wel hath formed him Nature
That I am his for ever, I him assure;   15
For every wight preyseth his gentilesse.

And notwithstondyng al his suffisaunce,
His gentil herte is of so gret humblesse
To me in word, in werk, in contenaunce,
And me to serve is al his besynesse,   20
That I am set in verrey sikernesse.
Thus oghte I blesse wel myn aventure,
Sith that him list me serven and honoure;
For every wight preiseth his gentilesse.

Now certis, Love, hit is right covenable   25
That men ful dere abye thy nobil thing,
As wake abedde, and fasten at the table,
Wepinge to laughe, and singe in compleynyng,
And doun to caste visage and lokyng,
Often to chaunge hewe and contenaunce,   30
Pleyne in slepyng, and dremen at the daunce,
Al the revers of any glad felyng.

Jelosie be hanged be a cable!
She wolde al knowe thurgh her espying.
Ther doth no wyght nothing so resonable,   35
That al nys harm in her ymagenyng.
Thus dere abought is Love in yevyng,
Which ofte he yiveth withouten ordynaunce,
As sorwe ynogh, and litil of plesaunce,
Al the revers of any glad felyng.   40

A lytel tyme his yift ys agreable,
But ful encomberous is the usyng;
For subtil Jelosie, the deceyvable,
Ful often tyme causeth desturbyng.
Thus be we ever in drede and sufferyng;   45
In nouncerteyn we languisshe in penaunce,
And han ful often many an hard mischaunce,
Al the revers of any glad felyng.

But certes, Love, I sey not in such wise
That for t'escape out of youre las I mente;   50
For I so longe have ben in your servise
That for to lete of wil I never assente;

No fors thogh Jelosye me turmente!
Sufficeth me to sen hym when I may;
And therfore certes, to myn endyng day,   55
To love hym best ne shal I never repente.

And certis, Love, when I me wel avise
On any estat that man may represente,
Then have ye maked me, thurgh your fraunchise,
Chese the best that ever on erthe wente.   60
Now love wel, herte, and lok thou never stente;
And let the jelous putte it in assay
That, for no peyne, wol I not sey nay;
To love him best ne shal I never repente.

Herte, to the hit oughte ynogh suffise   65
That Love so high a grace to the sente,
To chese the worthieste in alle wise
And most agreable unto myn entente.
Seche no ferther, neythir wey ne wente,
Sith I have suffisaunce unto my pay.   70
Thus wol I ende this compleynt or this lay;
To love hym best ne shal I never repente.

Lenvoy

Princesse, receyveth this compleynt in gre,
Unto your excelent benignite
Direct after my litel suffisaunce.   75
For elde, that in my spirit dulleth me,
Hath of endyting al the subtilte
Wel nygh bereft out of my remembraunce;
And eke to me it ys a gret penaunce,
Syth rym in Englissh hath such skarsete,   80
To folowe word by word the curiosite
Of Graunson, flour of hem that make in Fraunce.

Lenvoy de Chaucer a Scogan

Tobroken been the statutz hye in hevene
That creat were eternally to dure,
Syth that I see the bryghte goddis sevene
Mowe wepe and wayle, and passion endure,
As may in erthe a mortal creature.   5
Allas, fro whennes may thys thing procede,
Of which errour I deye almost for drede?

By word eterne whilom was yshape
That fro the fyfte sercle, in no manere,
Ne myghte a drope of teeres doun escape.   10
But now so wepith Venus in hir spere
That with hir teeres she wol drenche us here.
Allas! Scogan, this is for thyn offence;
Thow causest this diluge of pestilence.

Hastow not seyd, in blaspheme of the goddes,   15
Thurgh pride, or thrugh thy grete rekelnesse,
Swich thing as in the lawe of love forbode is,
That, for thy lady sawgh nat thy distresse,
Therfore thow yave hir up at Michelmesse?
Allas? Scogan, of olde folk ne yonge   20
Was never erst Scogan blamed for his tonge.

Thow drowe in skorn Cupide eke to record
Of thilke rebel word that thou hast spoken,
For which he wol no lenger be thy lord.

And, Scogan, though his bowe be nat broken,   25
He wol nat with his arwes been ywroken
On the, ne me, ne noon of oure figure;
We shul of him have neyther hurt ne cure.

Now certes, frend, I dreede of thyn unhap.
Lest for thy gilt the wreche of Love procede   30
On alle hem that ben hoor and rounde of shap,
That ben so lykly folk in love to spede.
Than shal we for oure labour han no mede;
But wel I wot, thow wolt answere and saye:
'Lo, olde Grisel lyst to ryme and playe!'   35

Nay, Scogan, say not so, for I m'excuse—
God helpe me so!—in no rym, dowteles,
Ne thynke I never of slep to wake my muse,
That rusteth in my shethe stille in pees.
While I was yong, I put hir forth in prees;   40
But al shal passe that men prose or ryme;
Take every man hys turn, as for his tyme.

Envoy

Scogan, that knelest at the stremes hed
Of grace, of alle honour and worthynesse,
In th'ende of which strem I am dul as ded,   45
Forgete in solytarie wildernesse,—
Yet, Scogan, thenke on Tullius kyndenesse;
Mynne thy frend, there it may fructyfye!
Far-wel, and loke thow never eft Love dyffye.

Lenvoy de Chaucer a Bukton

My maister Bukton, whan of Crist our kyng
Was axed what is trouthe or sothfastnesse,
He nat a word answerde to that axing,
As who saith, 'No man is al trewe,' I gesse.
And therfore, though I highte to expresse   5
The sorwe and wo that is in mariage,
I dar not writen of it no wikkednesse,
Lest I myself falle eft in swich dotage.

I wol nat seyn how that yt is the cheyne
Of Sathanas, on which he gnaweth evere;   10
But I dar seyn, were he out of his peyne,
As by his wille he wolde be bounde nevere.
But thilke doted fool that eft hath levere
Ycheyned be than out of prison crepe,
God lete him never fro his wo dissevere,   15
Ne no man him bewayle, though he wepe!

But yet, lest thow do worse, take a wyf;
Bet ys to wedde than brenne in worse wise.
But thow shal have sorwe on thy flessh, thy lyf,
And ben thy wives thral, as seyn these wise;   20
And yf that hooly writ may nat suffyse,
Experience shal the teche, so may happe,
That the were lever to be take in Frise
Than eft to falle of weddynge in the trappe.

This lytel writ, proverbes, or figure   25
I sende yow, take kepe of yt, I rede;
Unwys is he that kan no wele endure.
If thow be siker, put the nat in drede.
The Wyf of Bathe I pray yow that ye rede
Of this matere that we have on honde.   30
God graunte yow your lyf frely to lede
In fredam; for ful hard is to be bonde.

The Complaint of Chaucer to his Purse

To yow, my purse, and to noon other wight
Complayne I, for ye be my lady dere!
I am so sory, now that ye been lyght;
For certes, but ye make me hevy chere,
Me were as leef be layd upon my bere;   5
For which unto your mercy thus I crye:
Beth hevy ageyn, or elles mot I dye!

Now voucheth sauf this day, or yt be nyght,
That I of yow the blisful soun may here,
Or see your colour lyk the sonne bryght,   10
That of yelownesse hadde never pere.
Ye be my lyf, ye be myn hertes stere,
Quene of comfort and of good companye:
Beth hevy ageyn, or elles moot I dye!

Now purse, that ben to me my lyves lyght   15
And saveour, as doun in this world here,

Out of this toune helpe me thurgh your myght,
Syn that ye wole nat ben my tresorere;
For I am shave as nye as any frere.
But yet I pray unto your curtesye: 20
Beth hevy agen, or elles moot I dye!

Lenvoy de Chaucer

O conquerour of Brutes Albyon,
Which that by lyne and free eleccion
Been verray kyng, this song to yow I sende;
And ye, that mowen alle oure harmes amende,   25
Have mynde upon my supplicacion!

Against Women Unconstant

Balade

MADAME, for your newefangelnesse,
Many a servaunt have ye put out of grace.
I take my leve of your unstedfastnesse,
For wel I wot, whyl ye have lyves space,
Ye can not love ful half yeer in a place,   5
To newe thing your lust is ay so kene;
In stede of blew, thus may ye were al grene.

Right as a mirror nothing may enpresse,
But, lightly as it cometh, so mot it pace,
So fareth your love, your werkes bereth witnesse.   10
Ther is no feith that may your herte enbrace;

But, as a wedercok, that turneth his face
With every wind, ye fare, and that is sene;
In stede of blew, thus may ye were al grene.

Ye might be shryned, for your brotelnesse,   15
Bet than Dalyda, Creseyde or Candace;
For ever in chaunging stant your sikernesse;
That tache may no wight fro your herte arace.
If ye lese oon, ye can wel tweyn purchace;
Al light for somer, ye woot wel what I mene,   20
In stede of blew, thus may ye were al grene.

Complaynt D'Amours

An Amorous Complaint, Made at Windsor

I, WHICH that am the sorwefulleste man
That in this world was ever yit livinge,
And leest recoverer of himselven can,
Beginne right thus my deedly compleininge
On hir, that may to lyf and deeth me bringe,   5
Which hath on me no mercy ne no rewthe
That love hir best, but sleeth me for my trewthe.

Can I noght doon ne seye that may yow lyke?
Nay, certes! Now, allas! allas, the whyle!
Your plesaunce is to laughen whan I syke,   10
And thus ye me from al my blisse exyle.
Ye han me cast in thilke spitous yle
Ther never man on lyve mighte asterte;
This have I for I love you best, swete herte!

Sooth is, that wel I woot, by lyklinesse,   15
If that it were a thing possible to do
For to acompte youre beautee and goodnesse,
I have no wonder thogh ye do me wo;
Sith I, th'unworthiest that may ryde or go,
Durste ever thinken in so hy a place,   20
What wonder is, thogh ye do me no grace?

Allas! thus is my lyf brought to an ende;
My deeth, I see, is my conclusion.
I may wel singe, 'In sory tyme I spende
My lyf;' that song may have confusioun!   25
For mercy, pitee, and deep affeccioun,
I sey for me, for al my deedly chere,
Alle thise diden, in that, me love yow dere.

And in this wyse and in dispayr I live
In love; nay, but in dispayr I dye!   30
But shal I thus yow my deeth foryive,
That causeles doth me this sorwe drye?
Ye, certes, I! For she of my folye
Hath nought to done, although she do me sterve;
Hit is nat with hir wil that I hir serve!   35

Than sithen I am of my sorwe the cause,
And sithen I have this, withoute hir reed,
Than may I seyn, right shortly in a clause,
It is no blame unto hir womanheed
Though swich a wrecche as I be for hir deed.   40
Yet alwey two thinges doon me dye,
That is to seyn, hir beautee and myn yë;

So that, algates, she is array rote
Of my disese, and of my deth also;
For with oon word she mighte be my bote,   45

120

If that she vouched sauf to do so.
But than is hir gladnesse at my wo?
It is hir wone plesaunce for to take,
To seen hir servaunts dyen for hir sake!

But certes, than is al my wonderinge,   50
Sithen she is the fayrest creature
As to my doom, that ever was livinge,
The benignest and beste eek that Nature
Hath wrought or shal, whyl that the world may dure,
Why that she lefte pite so behinde?   55
It was, ywis, a greet defaute in Kinde.

Yit is al this no lak to hir, pardee;
But God or Nature sore wolde I blame.
For, though she shewe no pite unto me,
Sithen that she doth othere men the same,   60
I ne oughte to despyse my ladyes game;
It is hir pley to laughen whan men syketh,
And I assente, al that hir list and lyketh!

Yet wolde I, as I dar, with sorwful herte
Biseche unto your meke womanhede   65
That I now dorste my sharpe sorwes smerte
Shewe by word, that ye wolde ones rede
The compleynte of me, which ful sore I drede
That I have seid here, through myn unkonninge,
In any word to your displesinge.   70

Lothest of anything that ever was loth
Were me, as wisly God my soule save!
To seyn a thing through which ye might be wroth;
And, to that day that I be leyd in grave,
A trewer servaunt shulle ye never have;   75

And, though that I have pleyned unto you here,
Foryiveth it me, myn owne lady dere!

Ever have I been, and shal, how-so I wende,
Outher to live or dye, your humble trewe;
Ye been to me my ginning and myn ende,   80
Sonne of the sterre bright and clere of hewe;
Alwey in oon to love yow freshly newe,
By God and by my trouthe, is myn entente;
To live or dye, I wol it never repente!

This compleynte on seint Valentynes day,   85
Whan every foughel chesen shal his make,
To hir, whos I am hool, and shal alwey,
This woful song and this compleynte I make,
That never yit wolde me to mercy take;
And yit wol I evermore her serve   90
And love hir best, although she do me sterve.

Merciles Beaute

A Triple Roundel

YOUR yen two wol slee me sodenly;
I may the beautee of hem not sustene,
So woundeth hit thourghout my herte kene.

And but your word wol helen hastily
My hertes wounde, while that hit is grene,   5
   Your yen two wol slee me sodenly;
   I may the beautee of hem not sustene.

Upon my trouthe I sey you feithfully
That ye ben of my lyf and deeth the quene;
For with my deeth the trouthe shal be sene.   10
   Your yen two wol slee me sodenly;
   I may the beautee of hem not sustene,
   So woundeth it thourghout my herte kene.

II

So hath your beautee fro your herte chaced
Pitee, that me ne availeth not to pleyne;   15
For Daunger halt your mercy in his cheyne.

Giltles my deeth thus han ye me purchaced;
I sey you sooth, me nedeth not to feyne;
   So hath your beautee fro your herte chaced
   Pitee, that me ne availeth not to pleyne.   20

Allas! that Nature hath in you compassed
So greet beautee, that no man may atteyne
To mercy, though he sterve for the peyne.
   So hath your beautee fro your herte chaced
   Pitee, that me ne availeth not to pleyne;   25
   For Daunger halt your mercy in his cheyne.

III

Sin I fro Love escaped am so fat,
I never thenk to ben in his prison lene;
Sin I am free, I counte him not a bene.

He may answere, and seye this and that;   30
I do not fors, I speke right as I mene.
   Sin I fro Love escaped am so fat,
   I never thenk to ben in his prison lene.

Love hath my name ystrike out of his sclat,
And he is strike out of my bokes clene
For evermo; [ther] is non other mene.
  Sin I fro Love escaped am so fat,
  I never thenk to ben in his prison lene;
  Sin I am free, I counte him not a bene.

Proverbs

I

WHAT shul thise clothes thus manyfold,
  Lo! this hote somers day?—
After greet hete cometh cold;
  No man caste his pilche away.

II

Of al this world the large compas
  Hit wol not in myn armes tweyne,—
Whoso mochel wol embrace,
  Litel therof he shal distreyne.

COMMENTARY AND NOTES

Explanations of words given in these notes apply, exclusively or especially, to their immediate context. Explanations of general application will be found in the glossary at the end of the book.

p. 25 *The Romaunt of the Rose*

Standard editions of Chaucer's poems contain three separate fragments of this poem (a total of 7,700 lines). Only the first 1,705 lines are now considered to be by Chaucer and they have an obvious superiority to the remainder. There were many translations and adaptations during the fourteenth and fifteenth centuries of this popular thirteenth-century French metrical romance, of which the first part was by Guillaume de Lorris and the later continuation by Jean de Meun. The *Roman* is a dream poem in which the poet is invited by Idleness to enter a pleasure garden, where he meets a number of allegorical figures. He later falls in love with a rosebud mirrored in the fountain of Narcissus.

22-23 *taketh his cariage Of yonge folk*: receives fresh encouragement from young people.

28-29 There is nothing in that dream which did not afterwards take place.

36 Whether the enquirer be man or woman.

38 *hatte*: be called; *rede you here*: advise you to listen.

42 *in gree that she it take*: that she accepts it favourably.

54 *busk*: bush; *hay*: hedge.

55 *that it nil shrouded ben*: that is not covered (with leaves or flowers).

56 *wren*: covered.

67 *ynde and pers*: dark blue and light blue.

70 *to preisen is*: is worthy to be praised.

73 *gryl*: rough.

78 *myght*: best.

81 *chelaundre*: a kind of lark; *papyngay*: parrot.
91 *affraieth*: excites.
96 *wissh*: washed.
98 *aguler*: needle-case.
104 *bastyng*: tacking on
115 *stif*: strong.
118-19 And it was less in volume than the Seine but much broader.
129 *beet*: adjoined.
131 And very mild (without a doubt).
134 *costeiyng*: coasting.
137-8 *everydell Enclosed*: enclosed on every side.
140 *portraied*: painted with frescoes; *entailled*: carved.

148 *onde*: envy.
149 *moveresse*: stirrer up of quarrels.
150 *chideresse*: scold.
151 *fel corage*: spite.
154 *afraied*: distracted.
155 *Yfrounced*: wrinkled.
157 Her nose was distorted with vexation.
159 *rusty*: smeared, filthy.
160 *ywrithen*: swathed.

211 *caytif*: wretched.
214 *langour*: slow starvation.
216-17 *breed Kneden with eisel*: bread kneaded with vinegar; *egre*: sharp.
220 *courtepy*: cloarse short coat.
223 *Clouted*: patched up.
225 *perche*: wooden peg or bar.
226 *burnet*: of rough brown cloth.
227 *menyver*: miniver, a fur of fine quality.
235 *forwered*: worn out.

p. 31   The Book of the Duchess

The Duchess was Blanche, wife of Chaucer's patron, John of Gaunt. According to Robinson, the poem is 'almost the only production of Chaucer that can with confidence be attached to an actual occurrence'. Blanche, Duchess of Lancaster, died in 1369, and Chaucer's poem was composed soon afterwards in praise of her and in sympathy with the bereaved Duke. It was modelled on French poetic visions of love, and especially on the work of Guillaume Machaut. The poem is uneven in quality and far from successful throughout its 1,334 lines. But the passages given here show unmistakable signs of Chaucer's vivid imagination and growing command of verse.

298 *among*: all the while.
302 *servise*: musical performance.
309 *entewnes*: tunes.
310-11 And certainly I wouldn't have missed their singing for the city of Tunis.
318 *hym peyned*: took the trouble.
322 *depeynted*: painted.
324 *ycrased*: cracked.
333 *glose*: commentary.
346 *T'assay*: to try out, test.
351 *with strengthe*: 'in regular chase with horses and hounds' (Robinson).
353 *embosed*: become exhausted.
358 *stente*: stopped.
362 *relayes*: set of fresh horses or hounds; *lymeres*: tracking hound on leash.
365 *ladde*: who lead.
368 *Octovyen*: the Roman Emperor Octavian.
369 *faste*: near.
370 *A Goddes half*: In God's name; *in good tyme*: that's lucky.
374 Prepared everything necessary for hunting.
375 *fot-hot*: hotfoot, speedily.
376 *mot*: notes.
379 *Yhalowed*: Hallooed; *rechased*: chased.
381 *rused*: made a detour; *staal*: stole.
382 *privy*: secret.
384 And lost her scent.
385 *hunte*: huntsman.
386 *forloyn*: call to indicate that the quarry was far off.
390 *koude no good*: did not know what to do.
391 *lowe*: humbly.
392 *yknowe*: known.
398 *wente*: footpath.
400 *fele*: many.
402 *Flora*: goddess of flowers; *Zephirus*: the west wind.
405-6 For, to look at it, it seemed as if it strove to be gayer than heaven.
408 *swiche seven*: seven times more.
409 *welken*: sky; *sterres*: stars.

563 *glade*: gladden, lighten.

565 *lorn*: destroyed.

567 *slyde*: pass away.

568 The reference is to Ovid's *Remedia Amoris*.

570 *playes slye*: cunning contrivances.

572 Hippocrates was founder of Greek medicine, Galen a later medical authority.

574-6 But if anyone wishes to test himself to see whether he is capable of pity for another's sorrow, let him look at me.

579 *Yworthe*: become.

581 *be me loothe*: are loathsome to me.

582 *For al welfare*: this seems to go with the previous line, but the meaning is doubtful. *Wroothe*: angry.

583-4 Death itself is so much my enemy that it will not let me die – even though I want to.

587 *wythoute red*: helpless.

588 *deynge*: dying.

589 *Cesiphus*: Sisyphus in Greek mythology was condemned in Hades to the eternal punishment of rolling a stone up a hill, down which it rolled before it reached the top.

591-4 Anyone who knew all my sorrow, and had no pity and compassion for my grief would, I swear, have the heart of a fiend.

598 *the*: thee.

602 My leisure is spent in labour (pain).

603 *my wele is woo*: my pleasure is sorrow. (This whole passage is deliberately antithetical, continuously playing paradoxically on words.)

605 *pleynge*: rejoicing.

607 *hele*: health.

608 Doubt is my only certainty.

610 *wyt*: wisdom.

613 Of doubtful meaning – possibly 'My self-possession has turned to foolishness'.

614 And where I am is all confusion.

615 My peace is in contention and hostility.

616 *werre*: worse.

621 That promises all and performs nothing.

622 *halt*: is lame.

623 Hides a sidelong or crafty glance under a fair outside.

624 The cruel fair one.

627 *wrien*: betray.

628 *ywrien*: disguised.

629 Like filth bestrewn with flowers.

30-1 Her devotion is to lying, which is her chief excellence.

32 *mesure*: moderation.

35 What has been raised she casts down.

44 *whel*: wheel.

47 *yblent*: deceived.

48-9 She is a game of false magic, seeming to be one thing and being another.

53 *draughtes*: moves; *dyvers*: various.

54 She crept up on me and stole my queen. (Thus bringing about the end of the game.)

60 *in myd poynt of the chekker*: in the centre of the board.

61 *poun errant*: travelling pawn.

63 *Athalus*: Attalus III King of Pergamus in the second century B.C.

66 Had been able to solve the chess problems.

70 *And thogh wherto?* Yet to what purpose?

73 *kan*: is capable of.

82 I would have made the same move.

83 For, I hope a wise God will give me rest.

88 *holly*: wholly.

89 *turned*: destroyed.

90 *Be*: by

91 For there is nothing I desire.

95 That does not make me, each of them, a gift.

97 *avise me*: consider.

98 *every del*: in every way.

99-700 Meaning doubtful. Possibly 'How there is no means of reckoning up the sum of my sorrow'.

01 *leveth*: lives.

03 *suffisance*: contentment.

05 *ryght noght*: absolutely nothing.

08 *that*: what.

09 Tantale: 'Tantalus, in Greek mythology . . . is represented as punished in hell . . . by being set, thirsty and hungry, in a pool of water which recedes when he attempts to drink it, and under fruit-trees whose fruit he tries in vain to reach.' (*Oxford Companion to Literature*)

39   The House of Fame

is now usual to place this mysterious and – despite its length (2,158 lines) fragmentary poem at a comparatively early date. It has been assigned to period between 1374 and 1385, and probably before 1380. It may be

called mysterious because its purpose and meaning are still the subject c
scholarly contention. It begins as a love-vision, but the interest shifts t
Fame, by which is meant, not worldly glory, but rather Rumour – all th
is talked of by men and women throughout the world. Through his vis
to the House of Fame, situated between heaven and earth, Chaucer hope
to hear tidings, but what tidings it is never made quite clear. This un
certainty of intention, however, is not matched by any uncertainty of sty
or technique. The versification is fluent and assured; there is a remarkab
mastery of dialogue, and much graphic and picturesque detail. Above a
there is unmistakable evidence of Chaucer's characteristic predilection f
comedy. It has been pointed out that in *The House of Fame* Chaucer draw
on Latin and Italian sources – especially Virgil, Ovid and Dante. But wh
gives the poem the stamp of originality and individuality is its humorou
and satirical overtones, and its pervasive concern with the literary an
scientific interests of Chaucer's day. The passage which follows reveals th
golden Eagle as a comic 'guide, philosopher and friend', conducting
disarmingly naïf Chaucer to the House of Fame, instructing him like
benevolent but condescending pedant as he flies with him through th
upper air at the behest of his master, Jupiter.

664 To give you some amusement and diversion.
667-8 That you have paid to the undeserving and unregarding Cupid.
669-70 And so Jove, through his benevolent influence, will repay you i
some way.
672 *here*: hear.
674 *dar I leye*: I dare wager.
676 Both true sayings and false.
678 And love rewarded after long service.
679-81 And more loves begun by sheer chance, no one can tell why, just as
blind man rouses a hare (proverbial expression implying the extreme of luck
682-4 And more mirth and good speed, so long as they find love to be tru
as steel, as they think, and everything for the best.
686 *murmures*: complaints, whispering; *novelries*: change, fickleness.
688 And pretended reconciliations.
689 *berdys*: deceits (the proverbial phrase 'to make the beard' meant 't
delude').
691 *then greynes be of sondes*: than there are grains of sand.
692 *holdynge inhondes*: putting off with false promises.
693-4 And also more renewals of old abandoned relationships.
695 More days of reconciliation and agreement.
697 And also more exchange of endearments.
698 *graunges*: barns, granaries.

02 *to my wit*: so far as I can see.

03-6 That, even if Fame (Rumour) had all the magpies [the proverbial bearers of secrets] in a whole kingdom, and all its spies too, she could know all this, or they could spy it out.

06 *O yis, yis*: On the contrary.

08 *leve*: believe.

09 So long as you give your attention.

12 *thyn oune bok*: i.e. Ovid's *Metamorphoses*, in which the House of Fame is described.

17 *privy or apert*: in private or in public.

19 'And [it, the house] stands in so exactly determined a place' (Robinson).

22 Whether it is whispered, read or sung.

23 *suerte*: confidence, security.

24 Without doubt it must needs travel thither.

25 *for-why*: because.

26 *propre skille*: valid reason.

27 *worthy*: convincing.

30-2 That each existing natural thing has a natural place where it may best be preserved. References to this pre-Newtonian doctrine, by which every natural thing tends towards its natural place in the universe (as rivers to the sea, etc.), are common in medieval speculation, going back as far as St. Augustine.

37 *alday*: continually.

39 *wighte*: weight.

45-6 'While each of them is free ("at large"), a light thing seeks to go up and a heavy thing down.' (Robinson)

50 *by these skilles*: for these reasons.

56 In order that it should not deteriorate.

59 *daun*: Master (from *Dominus*).

60 *clerkys*: scholars.

64 *lere*: teach.

65 ff. This theory of the cause of sound was a commonplace, and Chaucer no doubt had read it in his favourite Boethius and elsewhere. It is by now becoming obvious, and will be made more so in Geoffrey's meek reply in line 864 to the intolerably patronising Eagle, that Chaucer is recording his sententious, repetitive and platitudinous exposition in a spirit of gentle mockery. This is a typically 'in' joke between Chaucer and his audience.

72 *devyse*: describe.

79 *tobreketh*: is shattered.

86 Because the House of Fame is the natural resting-place to which all sound tends by nature.

88 *experience*: experiment.

131

790 *anoon*: at once.

791 *roundell*: ripple (literally 'small circle').

792 Perhaps as broad as a pan lid.

794 *whel*: wheel, circle.

798 And so from small circle to great.

800 Causeth other ripples to be stirred up.

805 *under*: i.e. beneath the surface of the water.

807 *of trouthe I varye*: I am departing from the truth.

816 *leve*: dear.

823 *mynde*: memory, recollection.

824 *of pure kynde*: by sheer natural inclination.

826 This have I well proved, as you may understand by experiment.

840 *seweth*: follows.

847 *conservatyf*: retentive of.

850 As I first began to tell you.

858 *figures*: poetic figures of speech.

859 *colours*: fine phrases. In these lines the irony is obvious. Not only has the Eagle been extremely prolix but, as Clemen points out, he has used several devices from the medieval system of rhetoric. See note on line 765.

863 *attones*: all at once, at one and the same time.

866 Simply to a simple man.

867 *skiles*: reasons, arguments.

868-9 That he (the simple man) – so self-evident should they be – may shake them by the bills. (The Eagle naturally personifies ideas in terms of his own bodily form.)

875 *leve*: believe.

876 *or*: ere, before.

880 beginning and end in every detail.

884 *upper*: higher.

886 *game*: lighter things.

p. 46 *Anelida and Arcite*

This poem has been tentatively dated at about the same time as *The Parliament of Fowls* (i.e. about 1374). Much ink has been spilt over the questions of a possible topical reference to some incident in court life and of the sources of the poem. Little that is conclusive has come of it, except that Chaucer was indebted to Boccaccio's *Teseida* (from which the name 'Arcite' derives) and just possibly to Statius and Ovid. However, no source for the name 'Anelida' has been found. All this may amount to little more than an acknowledgment of Chaucer's originality,' for scholars are loath to credit anything to pure invention' (Robinson). This incomplete poem is justly admired for Anelida's *complainte d'amour* (beginning at line 169). The invocation and the beginning of the narrative suggests an intention, never fulfilled, to write a martial story like *Palamon and Arcite* in *The Canterbury Tales*. The stanza-form used in the complaint is one of the most elaborate ever used by Chaucer, and the lyric quality of the writing is remarkable.

1 *ferse*: fierce.

2 *Trace*: Thrace, where stood a temple to Mars.

5 *Bellona*: a Roman goddess of war. It is not clear why Pallas, the Greek god, is here linked to her.

6 *Be present*: this, like 'art honoured' in line 4, refers back to Mars in line 1.

6 *guye*: guide.

12-14 Which a long lapse of time (that can devour and eat up all things, as it has devoured many a noble story) has nearly eaten away from our memory.

15 *Polymyna*: Polyhymnia, one of the nine Muses.

16 *Parnaso*: Mount Parnassus, home of the Muses; *sustres*: sisters, i.e. the other eight Muses.

17 *Elycon*: Mount Helicon, supposed by Chaucer to be near Parnassus. Skeat thinks Chaucer confuses it with the Castalian spring. *Cirrea*: Cirra, an ancient town at the foot of Parnassus.

18 *memorial*: which records events.

19 *laurer*: laurel.

20 *do*: bring it about that. The metaphor for the completion of a task was common

21 *Stace*: Statius, author of the *Thebaid*, from Chaucer adapts part of the following passage. *Corynne*: Corinnus, said to have written a poem on Troy. The three lines in Latin following line 21 are from the *Thebaid*, Book XII. Chaucer adapts and expands them in lines 22-8.

23 *aspre*: fierce; *Cithe*: Scythia (cf. Shakespeare's 'barbarous Scythian' in *King Lear*).

24 *char*: chariot.

26 *al and somme*: each and all.

26 *sterres*: stars.

29 *duk*: duke, leader.

30 *trompes*: trumpeters.

32 *charge*: load.

33 *targe*: shield.

34 *route*: troop, company.

36 *Ipolita*: Hyppolita, Queen of the Amazons.

42 Filled with bounty and graciousness.

45 *Let I*: I will leave.

47-8 And now I will try to introduce craftily what I began to write about.

51 *fulfille*: satisfy – Juno was angry with the city of Thebes for having been the scene of some of her husband Jupiter's love affairs.

55 But forced his way, now here, now there, among both Greeks and Thebans.

56 *slough*: slew.

57-61 The names are those of combatants in the war of the Seven against Thebes.

63 'That no man knew of any remedy for his (own) misery.' (Skeat)

64 *Creon*: King of Thebes.

67 *dyde the gentils*: made the nobles.

69 *what*: whether.

72 *Ermony*: Armenia.

73 *that*: referring to Anelida.

76 *lyche*: like.

82 Penelope, wife of Odysseus, and Lucretia, wife of a noble Roman, were proverbial for their constancy.

83 *comprehended*: appraised, summed up.

84 *amended*: improved.

85 'The name of Arcite, which does not occur here in any of the mss., seems necessary to both sense and metre.' (Robinson)

87 *no thing pleyn*: devious.

90 For he assured her of his fidelity to such an extent.

93 *throwe*: short space of time.

94 *brast*: was bursting.

95 *bar hym lowe*: behaved humbly.

96 *wende have al his hert yknowe*: thought that she knew his whole heart.

98 *lere*: learn.

99 *mykel besynesse*: much trouble.

102 Or said he would go out of his mind.

103 *routhe and synne*: a piteous evil.

104 *wolde rewe*: chose to take pity.

105 A proverbial expression meaning 'The thoughts of a false man are nothing like those of a true one.'

106 Arcite found her liberality of such a kind.

108-9 she behaved towards nobody more pleasantly than was agreeable to Arcite.

110 *lak*: shortcoming; *wite*: reproach.

111 *ferforth yeven*: anxious.

112 That everything that pleased him pleased her.

114 *touched*: concerned.

115 *brent*: burnt.

116 *pleyn*: open, frank.

119 *bode*: delay; *heste*: command.

123 *evel apaid*: ill-disposed, angry.

124 Then she was afraid she would go out of her mind.

125 *sleght*: deceit.

127-8 She took all this so graciously that all his wishes seemed to her reasonable.

130 *as*: as if.

132 Her intention was so firmly set on fidelity.

135 That she scarcely took heed of what she ate.

138 *prevely*: secretly.

140 *dide her al this tene*: caused her all this trouble.

141 *newfanglenesse*: fondness for change.

143 *Tok lesse deynte of*: set less value on

145 *cladde him in her hewe*: dressed himself in the colours she affected (a common method of showing amorous interest).

147 *falsed*: betrayed.

149 *kynde of man*: man's nature.

150 *Lamek*: see *Genesis* IV 19, 'And Lamech took unto him two wives'.

154 'Chaucer curiously confounds him [Lamech] with Jabal, Lamech's *son*, who was "the father of such as dwell in tents".' (Skeat)

154 *but yf*: unless.

155 *sumwhat moste he feyne*: had to be somewhat deceitful.

156 *wex*: became.

157 The comparison is with a horse of uncertain temper which can either bite or whinny for attention.

158 For he made a false accusation against her of unfaithfulness.

161 *thef*: villain.

169 *swowneth*: swoons.

171 She falls into convulsions.

176 *mat*: exhausted.

177 *sustene*: support herself.

178 But continues to pine in this manner.

179 *nouther routhe ne tene*: neither pity nor concern.

182 He cares not whether she sink or swim.

183 *narowe*: tightly.

184 *stave*: shaft – the metaphor is of the lady's chariot, to which she keeps Arcite tightly harnessed.

186 *daunger*: domination.

187 *as her liste*: as she liked.

188 *lyvinge*: lifetime.

189 Any favour enough to cause him to sing for joy.

190-1 But drove him on, scarcely caring to acknowledge that he was her ladyship's (i.e. her own) servant.

193 *shipe*: reward.

197-8 Let all prudent women take note of the experience of Anelida and Arcite.

202 *straunge*: unyielding, hard to get; *also God me save*: as may God save me (one of Chaucer's rhetorical expletives).

208 *caste her for to make*: set about making.

211 *thirleth*: pierces (object, 'herte' in line 213).

212 *ywhet*: whetted.

214-5 That all my days of love are turned to fear and my carefree look into one of stupefaction.

218 *observaunce*: homage.

219 *til*: to; *Strophe*: this and *Antistrophe* are terms from Greek prosody, of little significance here.

222 *sithe*: times.

226 And his distress was instant death to me.

227 *ayein*: in return.

228 *kythe*: declare to be.

231 *ones*: once.

232 *pes*: peace.

233 *les*: snare.

237 *not*: know not.

238 *alas! the harde stounde*: O the bitter hour!

241 *founde*: search for.

242 *sounde*: heal.

243 *so ful yore*: so long ago.

244 *lore*: advice, instruction.

250 *awayting*: attentions.

253 *nother*: neither; *chere*: look, glance, sign.

254 By which you acknowledge my sadness?

258 *adversyte*: adversity.

259-60 Your good sense as a man ought to renounce the slaying of me your friend.

262-3 'Offended you, as surely as (I hope that) He who knows everything may free my soul from woe.' (Skeat)

267 *Myn honor save*: as far as in honour I could; *fre*: open, generous.

268 Therefore you hold this opinion of me.

272 *foo*: foe.

273 *furthered be your name*: your good name will be enhanced.

275 *sclaunder*: ill fame, disgrace.

276 *grame*: anger, grief, harm.

277 *God, wel thou wost*: as God well knows.

279 And then what is now amiss shall become a joke.

285 *departe*: divide, separate.

286 There is no middle course.

287 For as God will surely take pity on my soul.

289 *hewe*: colour, complexion.

294 I neglect any joy worth speaking of.

296 who may boast of greater sorrow.

299 And must I cast away my womanhood by begging to you?

301 And what need have I to ask for mercy, being guiltless?

304 *myne othes bede*: proffer my vows.

305 *mede*: reward.

306 Your manner is like a tree which bears flowers but no fruit.

309 I could as easily stop it raining in April.

315-16 Can an animal be said to be properly trained if it is liable to run away when least frightened?

317 Have mercy on me, dearest, if I speak falsely!

320 *Chaunte-pleure*: song of weeping – reference to a lost medieval poem.

322 *mased*: stunned with grief.

324 *good aventure*: good fortune.

328 And if I fall asleep for a few minutes (the time taken to walk a furlong or two).

330 *asure*: blue, the colour associated with faithfulness in love.

331 To proffer once more a new assurance (word-play on 'asure' in 330).

333 *drye*: suffer, endure.

334 And at daybreak I die from this dread.

338 But alas, your pity and your truth are too far to seek.

340-1 But my understanding is so weak that it will not extend to counsel or guide me out of this terror.

344 For I shall never again put in jeopardy my peace of mind.

346 *ful yore*: long ago.

347 *penaunce*: suffering.

350 Has pierced with the arrows of memory.

354 *a-swowe*: in a swoon.

357 *shapen*: constructed. The reason why the poem ends here, according to Skeat, is that the description of the Temple of Mars which was to follow appears in revised form in the *Knightes Tale*, 1109–1192.

Like *The Romaunt of the Rose* this poem, composed about 1382, is a love-vision based on the belief that on 14 February, St. Valentine's Day, the birds chose their mates. It owes much in general to the widespread medieval tradition of debate-poems, in which political and social satire is often found. But critics have praised it for its freshness of style, its originality, the vigour and naturalness of its dialogue (anticipating some of the best in *The Canterbury Tales*), and for its richness of literary allusion. Chaucer nowhere expresses more eloquently his love of books. H. S. Bennett notes the skill and care with which he has individualised the birds, and the evidence of his growing discontent with one of the subjects of his earliest concern as a poet – courtly love. Scholars have sought in vain for a historical event in Chaucer's time to which the poem may be related allegorically. The very variety of their conjectures is witness to the impossibility of regarding any conclusion in this matter as valid. It is perhaps enough to enjoy the poem for its intrinsic merits and to agree with some editors who are sceptical of any specific allegorical significance.

1 *craft*: i.e. of love

2 *th'assay*: the trial.

3 *slit so yerne*: slips away so soon.

7 I do not well know whether I sink or swim.

8 *al be*: although.

9 *quiteth folk here hyre*: rewards people for their services. In this and the following lines Chaucer explains that his experience of love is largely literary, rather than personal.

10 *happeth me*: it happens that I.

11 *yre*: ire, anger.

13-14 So keen are love's strokes that I dare only say 'God save me from such a master!' – I have no more to say.

15 From habit, whether for pleasure or for knowledge.

17-18 *Nat yoore Agon*: Not long ago.

19 *was write*: which was written.

21 All day I read it fast and eagerly.

25 *science*: knowledge; *lere*: learn.

26 But now to get to the point of all this.

28 *but a lyte*: very short.

31 The *Somnium Scipionis* of Marcus Tullius Cicero was preserved by Macrobius in a ms. of about A.D. 400 The *Somnium* (Dream), together with Macrobius' commentary, had considerable influence on medieval literature. The Scipio referred to is the younger Scipio Africanus, who visited Numidia about 150 B.C., where he talked of his father, the conqueror of Carthage by day and dreamed of him at night.

35 I will give you the essentials of his theme.

37 *Massynisse*: Masinissa, King of Numidia.

38 *inome*: taken.

40 *gan mysse*: came to an end.

41 *auncestre*: ancestor, i.e. Scipio Africanus the elder.

43 *a sterry place*: a starry place, i.e. heaven.

45-9 And forewarned him out of kindness, telling him that any well conducted man, learned or unlearned, who cared for the general good would attain to a place of bliss where lasting joy is to be found.

53 And that our span of life in this world.

58 In comparison with heaven's extent.

59 *the nyne speres*: the concentric orbits of the seven planets, the fixed stars and the *primum mobile* (motive power of the whole cosmos). In medieval cosmology the earth was at the centre and the rotation of the spheres was accompanied by music inaudible to human ears but now made audible to Scipio in his dream.

61 *thryes thre*: thrice three.

62 *welle*: source.

65 *harde grace*: misfortune.

67-8 'The reference is to the so-called Great or Mundane Year, the period in which all the heavenly bodies should depart from and return to a given position.' (Robinson)

69 *al shulde out of mynde*: all should be forgotten.

74 And always see to it that you work and teach.

77 *cleere*: noble, free.

79 *likerous*: lecherous.

82 *foryeven*: forgiven (note the similarity of this idea from Cicero to the Christian concept of Purgatory).

86 *reveth*: takes away; *bestes*: beasts.

88 *dresse*: prepare.

89 *Fulfyld*: full; *hevynesse*: sadness.

90-1 Both because I had something I did not want and also because I lacked something I wanted.

93 *For wery*: because weary (or simply, wearied).

94 *Tok:* took.

95 *as that*: as, while.

96-7 How Scipio Africanus (the elder) in the selfsame array as Scipio (his son) had seen him in.

100 *wode*: the wood.

103 *fon*: foes.

104 *syke*: sick man; *tonne*: cask.

110 *totorn*: much torn.

111 *roughte*: cared.

112 *quyte*: repay.

113 *Cytherea*: Venus, goddess of love.

114 Who subduest whom thou wilt with thy flaming torch (of love).

115 *sweven*: dream.

117 as surely as I saw thee (as a star) in the north-north-west.

119 *t'endyte*: to compose.

120 *hente*: caught hold of.

122 *grene ston*: i.e. mossy stone.

125 *difference*: the verses on either half of the gateway give contrasting or contradictory advice.

127 *Thorgh*: through.

128 *Of hertes hele*: Where hearts are healed.

131 *aventure*: fortune.

136 *Daunger*: power to harm.

138 *were*: weir.

140 The only remedy is to avoid it.

142 *gan astoned to beholde*: beheld with astonishment.

144 *bolde*: grow bold.

145 The first warmed me, the second chilled me.

146 Through doubt I had no knowledge of how to choose.

147 *flen*: to flee; *lese*: lose.

148 *adamauntes*: lodestones.

150 *meve*: move.

151 For whatever one may attract the other prevents (from moving).

152-3 I was so placed (i.e. like the piece of iron), not knowing whether it was better for me to enter or to leave.

154 *shof*: pushed.

158 *nis nothyng ment bi the*: is not intended for thee.

161 *sek*: sick.

163 *Yit that*: what.

164 *pul*: throw.

166 And judge whether this wrestler or that does the better.

167 *connyng*: skill, knowledge.

168 I will show you matter to write about.

171 *wel begoon*: had made a good start.

176-82 'Lists of trees, such as the one here given, are a well-known convention in classical and modern poetry', according to Robinson, who also mentions parallels in Ovid and Boccaccio, quoting the following from the medieval writer, Joseph of Exeter: 'fraxinus audax' (*the hardy asshe*), 'cantatrix buxus' (*the box-tree pipere*), 'cupressus flebilis' (*the cypresse, deth to playne*), 'oliva concilians' (*the oliyve of pes*), 'ebria vitis' (*the dronke vyne*), 'interpres laurus' (*the laura to devyne*).

The following is a paraphrase of Chaucer's catalogue of trees: The builder oak and also the hardy ash, the pillar elm (because sometimes used for propping up vines), used as coffins for bodies, the box tree (used for turning wooden pipes), handle★ to the whiplash, the sailing fir (because used for masts), the cypress, symbol of mourning for the dead, the yew as used for shooting, the aspen for smooth arrows, the olive of peace, and also the drunken vine, the palm of victory and the laurel used in divination.

★ I take *holm* in line 178 to be the same as the modern 'haulm', a stalk, and not the holm or evergreen oak. The scholars are silent on this point.

185 Where there is evermore much sweetness.

188 *smale*: slender; *lighte*: nimble (or nimbly).

192 Some were occupied in breeding more birds.

193 *conyes*: rabbits.

195 *dredful*: timid.

197 *strenges*: strings.

201 *unnethe it myghte be lesse*: it could scarcely be less.

204 *attempre*: temperate.

212 *Forge and file*: verbs governing 'arwes'.

214 *Wille*: Cupid's daughter is either Will or, some editors think, Voluptuousness.

215 *heveds*: heads.

217 *kerve*: carve, cut.

218 Then was I straightway aware of.

219 *Aray*: Comeliness.

220-1 And of the Craft that has the power to force a man to commit follies (presumably Love as an art or game).

222 *Disfigurat*: disguised.

228 *Messagerye, and Meede*: Sending of Messages, and Reward. It is not clear who the 'other thre' are.

232 *daunseden*: danced.

234 *gay*: finely dressed.

235 *kertels*: skirts; *dishevele*: with hair hanging loosely.

236 *offyce*: occupation, function.

240 *curtyn*: presumably a piece of embroidery.

244-5 And nearby, both inside and outside the temple, I found Artful Requests and a train of their followers.

246-7 Within the temple I heard a murmuring noise of sighs as hot as fire that arose on all sides.

249 *auter*: altar; *brenne*: burn.

251 *drye*: endure.

253 *Priapus*: god of fertility. According to Ovid, he was disconcerted (*shente*) by the braying of an ass in the night.

257 *assaye and fonde*: two verbs meaning 'endeavour'.

260 *disport*: pleasure, amusement, sport.

262 *hautayn of hire port*: of proud demeanour.

263-4 The place was dark, but later I saw light for a time, though it could scarcely have been dimmer.

271 *remenaunt*: rest, remainder (of her body); *to my pay*: to my satisfaction.

272 Just with a thin cloth from Valence (in France, noted for its silk trade).

273 *defense*: covering.

274 *sote*: sweet.

276 *boote*: remedy. Ceres in Roman mythology was the goddess of the harvest.

277 *Cypride*: the Cyprian, i.e. Venus.

279 *To ben here helpe*: to come to their aid.

281-4 That, in spite of the efforts of Diana, goddess of chastity, many a broken bow hung on the wall (as symbols of Venus' triumph) belonging to maidens who had wasted their time in the service of Diana.

286 *Calyxte*: Callisto, whom Juno, jealous of her beauty, changed into a she-bear, after which she was raised to heaven as the constellation Ursa Major. *Athalante*: Atalanta, in Greek mythology a famous huntress who married Hippomenes who defeated her in a foot-race.

287 *wante*: lack.

288-92 A catalogue of lovers in classical, eastern and Celtic legend who were unfortunate in love.

297 I then walked forth to comfort myself.

299-300 Who, just as the summer sunshine surpasses the stars in brightness.

302 *launde*: glade, clearing.

305 *cast*: design; *mesure*: plan.

306-8 There was no bird in creation but was prompt in her service, to receive her judgement and listen to her.

310 *chese his make*: choose his mate.

316 *Aleyn*: Alanus de Insulis, twelfth-century author of the inordinately long *Planctus Naturae (Complaint of Nature)*.

317 describes the dress and appearance of nature.

321 *woned*: wont, accustomed.

323-9 Chaucer's fourfold division into birds of prey, birds which eat worms etc., water-fowl and seed-eaters is derived ultimately from Aristotle.

327 *the dale*: i.e. the glade referred to in line 302.

329 *fele*: many.

331 Who with his keen gaze pierces the sun – a metaphorical reference to the

proverbial idea that the eagle has a special capacity to look straight at the sun
334 *tiraunt*: tyrant; *donne*: dun, brown.
335-6 *doth pyne To*: does harm to, torments; *ravyne*: gluttony.
337 *distrayneth*: clutches, grasps.
338 *hardy sperhauk*: bold sparrow-hawk.
339 *merlioun*: merlin, small hawk.
342 *jelous*: suspicious, protective (of its young) – the reference is to the proverbial belief in the 'swan song'.
343 *bode*: foreboding, prophecy, omen.
344 *the geaunt, with his trompes soun*: the giant with his trumpeting cry.
345 *janglynge pye*: chattering magpie.
346 *skornynge jay*: The jay was thought to mock at the owl when abroad by day.
347 Lapwings adopt deceptive procedures during the incubation of their young, to distract the attention of possible marauders.
348 *stare*: starling – which, because it can talk, was thought to betray secrets.
349 *ruddok*: robin.
350 The cock, who is timepiece to small villages.
351 'The sparrow was sacred to Venus, from its amatory disposition.'(Skeat)
352 *clepeth*: calls – the songing of the nightingale was supposed to coincide with the budding of the trees.
353 *mortherere*: murderer; *foules smale*: here, tiny winged creatures, i.e. insects.
355 *turtil*: the turtle-dove, proverbially faithful in love.
356 *aungels fetheres*: The feathers of angels' wings were often represented in medieval art as resembling those of peacocks.
357 It has been suggested that Chaucer here means that the pheasant, by breeding with the domestic hen, makes a cuckold – an object of scorn – of the cock.
358 *waker goos*: 'The Goose likewise is very vigilant and watchfull: witnesse the Capitoll of Rome, which by the means of Geese was defended and saved.' (Holland's Pliny)
358 *unkynde*: unnatural, because of the manner in which it raises its young at the expense of other birds.
359 The parrot, full of wantonness.
360 The drake or mallard is said to destroy its young unless removed.
361 *wreakere of avouterye*: avenger of adultery. 'The story is that a male stork, having discovered that the female was unfaithful to him, went away; and presently returning with a great many other storks, the avengers tore the criminal.' (Skeat)
362 *hote*: voracious – the cormorant was noted for gluttony.
363 The raven was thought wise because it could predict. *care*: anxiety – because the crow was a bird of ill omen.

364 *throstil*: the throstle was supposed to live to a great age. The fieldfare is seen in Britain in winter, departing with the warm weather.

366 *Stature*: the editors do not explain this. I suggest 'shape' or 'identity'.

369 *dide his besy cure*: was actively employed.

371 *formel*: fit companion; *make*: mate.

666 *This werk*: i.e. the choosing of their mates by the birds.

668 *evene acord*: common agreement.

670-1 'They embraced each other with their wings and by intertwining their necks.' (Skeat)

672 *kynde*: nature.

675 *roundel*: a short song-like poem based on one of various French models, Chaucer's favourite being the one beginning at line 468. It has two rhymes only and involves the repetition of the first three lines.

677 *note*: melody.

681 *wedres*: storms; *overshake*: shaken off.

683 *on-lofte*: aloft, i.e. in heaven.

687 *gladen*: rejoice.

688 *recovered*: obtained.

689 *mowe*: may.

696 *yit*: yet, still.

697-9 These lines, typical of Chaucer's devotion to literature, may be paraphrased: I hope that by continually reading I shall come across something some day which will help me to prosper.

p. 73 Troilus and Criseyde

Troilus and Criseyde is a poem in five books, averaging about 1,700 lines each. The verse form is that of the *rime royal* stanza: seven iambic pentameters rhyming *a b a b b c c*. Unique in English literature, it has been called 'the first modern novel'. It concerns the failure of Troilus' romantic love affair with Criseyde through her enforced withdrawal from Troy to the camp of the besieging Greeks. The three principal characters are portrayed with a psychological penetration unprecedented in English poetry – Criseyde's uncle, Pandarus, the worldling and realist who engineers the affair; Troilus, the brave soldier and star-crossed lover, loyal to the tradition of chivalric *amour courtois*; and Criseyde, one of the most complex of Chaucer's women, at once a romantic and a realist. But *Troilus and Criseyde* is neither a novel nor a discussion of chivalric and Christian ideas: it is first and foremost a poem, concerned with the pathos, the humour, and the irony of men and women in love.

Much scholarly discussion has been occupied with Chaucer's sources, of which the chief is Boccaccio's *Filostrato*, and with possible allusions to life at the English court during the period of composition (about 1385). What emerges most clearly, however, is Chaucer's miraculous originality, both in his treatment of the story and the characters and in the beauty of his language and versification.

It is impossible to give an adequate idea of this astonishing major work in necessarily very limited extracts. The five given here are chosen, not to summarise the narrative, but to illustrate Chaucer's poetic power – above all, his capacity to keep suspended in the fluid solution of his mature verse the complementary and conflicting elements of the pathos, the pity and the sense of irony which his characters and their situation evoke.

Criseyde's Dream
Book II lines 904–31
Criseyde, preoccupied with the revelation by Pandarus of Troilus' love for her, has been talking of love with her women in the garden.
906 *wrye*: turn.
908 *wexen*: become; *donne*: dun, dusky.
910 *yfeere*: together.
912 *voiden*: depart.
914 *til*: to.
915 *hust*: hushed, silent.
917 It is not necessary to relate, for you know it already.
920 Sang loud and full with its breast towards the moon.
921 *Peraunter*: peradventure, perhaps.
923 *in good entente*: attentively.
924 *hente*: seized, overcame.
925 *anonright tho*: immediately.
929 And placed his heart in her breast.
930 At which she felt neither fear nor pain.

Pandarus and Criseyde
Book III lines 1555–75
The morning after Troilus and Criseyde have first become lovers at his house, Pandarus comes to Criseyde's bedside to enjoy her discomfiture and, vicariously, her pleasure. This revelation of Pandarus' nature is one of Chaucer's psychological masterstrokes.
1555 *o-morwe*: in the morning.

1559 *laiser*: leisure – Pandarus' sly innuendo is typical of his indirect method of approach.

1563 *mury*: merry.

1566 *fare*: 'goings-on'. (Skeat)

1567 *white*: innocent-sounding.

1569 *wrye*: cover.

1572 *if that I shal be ded*: if you want to kill me.

Troilus and Criseyde Parted
Book V lines 666–714

Criseyde, after promising to return to Troy, has departed to the Greek camp at the command of her father, Calchas, who has defected to the Greeks. Troilus eats out his heart as he gazes towards the enemy tents where Criseyde too is in despair because her father will not let her return to Troy.

667 *the Grekis oost*: the Greek host.

670 *ther*: where.

672 *boote*: comfort.

673 *hardily*: certainly.

674 *stoundemele*: hour by hour.

675 *sikes*: sighs.

676 *preve*: prove by experience.

678 *sowneth so lik peyne*: has the sound of such distress.

679 *twynned*: parted.

680 *dryveth forth*: continued.

686 *stynten*: bring to an end.

690-1 *longe After*: long for.

691 *to*: too.

693 *wende*: imagined.

694-5 Nothing will induce my father to favour me with leave to return, wheedle him as I may.

696 *my terme pace*: outstay my promised time (i.e. ten days).

699 *unthonk*: no thanks.

700 *so weilaway the tide*: alas the day.

701 *me putte in jupartie*: take the risk.

703 *holde*: taken for.

706 *al be myn herte trewe*: although my heart is true.

707 *rewe*: take pity.

708 *ywoxen was*: had become.

709 *lymes*: limbs; *lene*: weak.

710 *the place*: i.e. Troy.

713 *despeired, out of alle cure*: in despair and beyond all remedy.

Book V lines 1107–76

On the tenth day of Criseyde's absence Troilus walks on the walls of Troy in a fever of impatience for her return. Pandarus the realist hides his own misgivings for the sake of his friend.

107 *Phebus*: Phoebus, the sun god in Roman mythology.

109 To warm the wet waves of the eastern sea. It is not clear what sea, if any, is meant precisely. There may be a hint here of parody of the grand style in poetry.

110 And the bird Ciris (possibly the lark), daughter of Nisus, sang with renewed vigour.

112 *pleyde*: passed the time.

117 *knowen hym aright*: recognise him (or her).

119 *byjaped*: made a mock of (because to the passers-by Troilus and Pandarus seemed to be staring at nothing).

124-5 It seems to me that she certainly has plenty to do to get away from her father.

126 *to dyne*: i.e. take her midday meal.

127 *pyne*: torment.

129 *forthi*: therefore.

133 *that they after gape*: what they are looking for.

134 Fortune itself thinks to trick them both.

138 *yate*: portcullis.

139 These gatekeepers were always ignorant.

141 As if there were no special reason, in case she comes late.

144 *greve*: grove.

145 *leyde*: stretched.

147 *menyng*: intention.

148 I was beginning to think my anguish was coming on me afresh.

149 *kan hire good*: will manage somehow.

151 *by myn hood!*: a more or less meaningless expletive.

152 *nycely*: foolishly.

153 *Gaure*: gape.

155 Don't think it, dear friend, tedious to wait.

157 *woltow trowen*: will you trust.

158 *Have here my trouthe*: Believe me.

160 *so mote I the!*: so may I thrive (i.e. so help me God!).

162 *fare-carte*: provision wagon.

166 My thoughts are towards something hopeful. (There is pathos in Troilus' invincible wishful thinking. Chaucer's psychological insight is far in advance of his time, at any rate in England.)

167 *Not I nat how*: I don't know how.

1171 And agreed with him in all he said.

1172 *softe lough*: laughed to himself.

1174-5 *abidest*: expect, hope for – Pandarus' ironical meaning is that his hope will not be fulfilled. The reference to 'joly Robyn' in the wood is to some now forgotten piece of folklore or folksong.

1176 *ferne yere*: last year – Pandarus' meaning is that Criseyde's love is as irrevocably lost as last year's snow. This phrase is also proverbial. Cf. 'Mais où sont les neiges d'antan' in the *Ballade des Dames du Temps Jadis* by François Villon (b. 1431), unforgettably translated by D. G. Rossetti: 'Where are the snows of yesteryear?'

Criseyde's Letter to Troilus
Book V lines 1590–1631
Among the Greeks Criseyde has already been unfaithful to Troilus with her smooth young protector Diomede, but she takes pity on Troilus and writes to him.

1590 *ensample of goodlyhede*: pattern of perfection.

1591 *sours of gentilesse*: fountain-head of nobility.

1593 *heleles*: out of health.

1596 I can send you neither courage nor comfort.

1597 *ypleynted*: covered with complaints.

1598 Have aroused pity in my heart.

1599 *teris*: tears; *depeynted*: stained.

1600 *requeren*: beg.

1605 *haste*: impatience.

1610 I am only delaying for fear of scandal.

1611-13 For I have heard more about how things stood between us than I thought was known, and I shall put this right by pretence.

1615 *holden me in honde*: try to coax me back.

1616-17 But no matter – I can only think that you are acting from wholly true and noble motives.

1618 *disjoynte*: a difficult situation.

1620 *apoynte*: say for certain.

1621-2 But indeed, I beg you as best I can for your approval and your friendship for always.

1623 *dure*: last.

1624 *ye may in me assure*: you can rely on me.

1625 *on yvel ye ne take*: not to take it ill.

1628 *endite*: write letters.

1629 But a great deal can be said in a small space.

1630 It is the thought that counts – not the length of the letter.

Envoy

Book V lines 1786–1870

Few things in Chaucer are more characteristic than this *Envoy*. Some of its contents – e.g. the request to other writers for criticism and correction (lines 1856 ff.) – are conventions of the time. Nevertheless Chaucer makes even such conventional usages all his own. The renunciation of worldly love in favour of divine felicity comes as something of a surprise to the modern reader, and scholars have disputed whether it is consistent with the poem as a whole. This too, although a familiar contemporary commonplace, must be accepted as sincere in view of its convinced poetic intensity.

1787-8 Whereas may God send strength to your author to engage in writing some tale with a happy ending.

1789-90 But little book, show no hatred to any other writing, but be humble before all poetry.

1792 *Omer*: Homer; *Stace*: Statius.

1793 *diversite*: i.e. pronunciation.

1796 *mysmetre*: misread, scan wrongly – according to Skeat, Chaucer is revealing in his fear that his lines may be wrongly stressed the knowledge that his English is somewhat archaic.

1797 *red . . . song*: i.e. read to himself by one person or recited before a company in an intuned voice.

1799 But let me go back to what I was saying before.

1801 *the Grekis boughten deere*: cost the Greeks dear.

1803-4 For I have never heard that he had an equal except Hector.

1805 *weilawey*: alas – the meaning of this line appears to be something like 'It would be a sad thing were it not the will of God' (the editors do not offer an explanation).

1806 Fierce Achilles mercilessly slew him (Troilus).

1808 *goost*: spirit.

1809-10 Up to the inside surface of the eighth sphere, leaving behind him the earthy elements of his nature. Some mss. have 'seventh' for 'eighth', but Chaucer follows Boccaccio in committing Troilus' spirit to the eighth of the celestial spheres, that of the moon. In medieval cosmology the earth was thought to be at the centre of a system of nine spheres – orbits of the various celestial bodies.

1811 *avysement*: contemplation.

1812 *erratik sterres*: planets. (See note to *The Parliament of Fowls*, line 59.)

1814 *avyse*: contemplate.

1818 In comparison with the pure delight.

1820 He looked down upon the place where he had been slain.

1821 *lough right*: laughed even.

1822 *faste*: bitterly.

1823 *dampned*: scorned.

1825 *sholden*: 'and we ought; *we* is understood.' (Skeat)

1827 To the dwelling-place allotted him by Mercury (presumably because Mercury was the messenger of the Gods).

1828 *fyn*: end, result.

1830 *estat real*: royal rank – Troilus was a son of Priam, King of Troy.

1832 *brotelnesse*: brittleness, frailty.

1837 *Repeyreth hom*: Return homewards (i.e. to your spiritual destiny).

1840 *faire*: a passing show – the comparison of life on earth to a mere fair is proverbial (cf. Hoccleve as quoted by Skeat: 'This lyf, my sone, is but a cheryfeyre.').

1842 *right*: just.

1843 *crois*: cross; *beye*: ransom, redeem.

1844 *starf*: died; *roos*: rose.

1845 *falsen*: betray, deceive.

1846 Who will set his heart entirely on Christ.

1848 What need is there to seek after false (worldly) loves?

1849 Consider old accursed pagan rites.

1852 *fyn and guerdoun*: end and reward; *travaille*: labour.

1853 *rascaille*: a gang (i.e. the pagan gods).

1854-5 If you read the writings of classical scholars, this is the sort of poetry you will find. (There seems to be here a note of sarcasm against the works of pagan authors.)

1856 *moral Gower*: this epithet, referring to the didactic character of Gower's verse, has stuck. John Gower (?1330–1408), author of the *Confessio Amantis* and other poems, was a friend of Chaucer.

1857 *Strode*: probably Ralph Strode, an Oxford philosopher and theologian, who was a fellow of Merton before 1360.

1858-9 To confirm, and where necessary to correct (what this book says), through your kindness and zeal for truth.

1860 And to Christ who was devoted to truth and died on the cross.

1861 *of*: for.

1863 Thou ever-living trinity.

1864 *regnest*: reignest.

1865 And who, thyself unbounded, yet containest all else.

1866 *foon*: foes.

1867 *to*: by

1868 *digne*: worthy.

1869 For the love of thy kindly Virgin Mother.

The Legend of Good Women, in the form of a love-vision, is a palinode – that is, an apology, in the shape of a celebration of women faithful in love, for alleged attacks on faithless women in *Troilus and Criseyde* and *The Romaunt of the Rose*. The stories themselves, of which one representative sample is given here, are not for the most part inspired, and it has been suggested that Chaucer was not particularly interested in them. This lends support to the possibility that he may have been urged to write the *Legend* at the behest of a patron. Most of the poetry of the *Legend* is in the *Prologue*, and readers have universally admired the famous celebration of the daisy. Several sources have been found for much of this *Prologue* in foreign literature, but its freshness and gaiety are Chaucer's own. His country scene is a living piece of England, not a literary rehash.

There are two texts, of which Robinson takes the one given here to be the earlier. This is preferred to the other, which seems to be a tidying-up, but leaves out some of the poetry. It is also to be noted that in the *Legend* Chaucer makes the first use in English of the rhymed decasyllabic couplet he later used in *The Canterbury Tales*. Chaucer's expression (lines 17 ff.) of passionate concern for books and scholarship is a real utterance from his heart and considerably strengthens the suggestion that his Clerk of Oxford is in some respects a self-portrait.

The Prologue
lines 1–269

9 *assay*: experience; *preve*: prove, test.

10–11 But God forbid that men should not believe many more things than they have seen with their eyes.

13 *But yf*: Unless.

15 *Thogh*: Even though.

16 *Bernard*: Bernard of Clairvaux (1091–1153) was famous for his learning.

17 *mote*: must go.

19 *wyse*: ways.

22 *regnes*: realms.

24 *rehersynges*: recital.

29 *konne*: know.

35-6 A later version has, in place of these lines:

> But it be other upon the halyday,
> Or ellis in the joly tyme of May

40 *condicioun*: temperament, disposition.

48 *ayein the sonne sprede*: opened towards the sun.

51-2 *have presence Of it*: am in its presence.

55 *evere ilyke*: always equally.

56 *and ever ylike newe*: 'and ever (do so) equally anew, i.e. unalterably.' (Skeat)

58 Although I take no oath on it, I will not lie about this.

60 *blyve*: as soon as possible.

64 *chere*: face.

69 *make of sentement*: write poems about your feelings.

71 *forthren*: further, assist.

72 A reference to the contemporary courtly mock-dispute between the upholders of the flower, representing the perishable beauty of young love, and those of the leaf, representing the more permanent virtues, such as constancy. Chaucer, with shrewd characteristic prudence, declines to take sides. The somewhat tedious fifteenth-century poem, *The Flower and the Leaf*, is thought to have been based on this passage in Chaucer.

73-5 'For I well know, that ye (poets) have long ere this reaped the field of poetry, and carried away the corn from it; and I come after you as a gleaner.' (Skeat) This passage was evidently intended to be taken with a big pinch of salt, but it is seldom demonstrable with certainty whether Chaucer's tongue is in his cheek or not. This equivocal tone is one of the hallmarks of Chaucer's poetry and an integral part of its indefinable charm.

78 And though it may often happen that I repeat.

79 *That*: What.

80 Bear with me and do not be angry.

85 *wynt*: guides.

86 *in-with*: within; *yow dredeth*: holds you (the daisy) in awe.

88 *and nothing I*: and not I myself.

89 *knyt so in youre bond*: so bound up in your service.

90 The beauty of this simile has been noted by the scholars, who for once have failed to find a foreign source for it.

95 I invoke you as my earthly deity.

97 But the reason why I told you (the reader) to believe in.

103 *besy gost*: ever-active spirit.

105 *gledy*: glowing, burning.

109 *dredful*: awestruck.

112 *beste*: the Bull (i.e. the sun was in the constellation of Taurus).

114 The reference is to the story in Greek mythology of Europe, who was carried off by Zeus in the guise of a white bull.

115 *anoon-ryght*: forthwith, at once.

116 *grette*: greeted.

119 *enbrouded*: embroidered, adorned.

121 *gomme*: gum, resin.

126 *mat*: dead.

128 *atempre*: temperate, mild; *releved*: revived.

130 *fayn*: fond.

131 *panter*: a kind of fowling net.

132 *awhaped*: terrified.

134 *In his dispit*: in scorn of him.

135 *despise*: throw contempt on.

136 *cherl*: villain; *coveytise*: greed.

137 *sophistrye*: cunning malice.

141 *make*: mate.

144 they continually returned to the subject of their pleasure. (Commentators do not explain 'turned', but this seems to be the general meaning.)

145 *Seynt Valentyn*: see introductory note to *The Parliament of Fowls* (p. 138).

152 Interpret that how you will – it's not my business. (A characteristic Chaucerian innuendo.)

153 *thoo*: those.

154 *tydif*: a small bird (possibly the wren); *for newfanglenesse*: for the sake of variety.

158 *rewe*: take pity.

159 *maden hire acord*: composed their differences.

160-2 'Although Daunger (i.e. power to harm or to repel) seemed for a time to have the upper hand, yet at the last Pity induced relenting, and caused Mercy to surpass (or prevail over) Right (or Justice).' (Skeat)

163 *ruled*: well-mannered.

164-6 But I do not call either folly or undeserved pity by the name of innocence, for virtue lies in moderation, as Aristotle says in his *Ethics* – that's what I mean.

168-9 Dedicated themselves to love and gave up the vice of hate.

171 *Zepherus and Flora*: in Roman mythology the west wind and his wife, goddess of flowers.

180 *shoop for me*: prepared, purposed.

186 *faire mote she falle*: she may have good luck

188-9 But nevertheless, do not think that, in praising the flower, I write against the leaf (see note to line 72).

191 For as for me, I like the one as well as the other.

192 I am not yet committed to the service of either.

193 *Ne I not*: Neither do I know.

194 *Wel browken they*: May they enjoy.

195 For my poem is concerned with something quite different (literally, out of another barrel. Chaucer was a vintner's son.)

196 *stryf*: i.e. the courtly disputation between upholders of the flower and of the leaf.

202 *devyse*: describe.

203 *herber*: arbour.

204 Which was provided with benches set on freshly laid turves.

206 For the sake of the pleasure of early summer

208 *hed*: hidden, closed.

211 *this flour*: i.e. the daisy; *drede*: revere.

212 *afer*: afar.

214 *real*: royal.

215 *fret of gold*: head-dress of gold wire; *heer*: hair.

217 *flourouns*: petals.

219 *leves lyte*: small petals.

221 *o perle fyn, oriental*: a single stone of highest quality.

223-5 Chaucer's repetitive elaboration of his description gives importance and emphasis to the queen's likeness to the daisy.

227 *greves*: sprays.

228 *fret*: ornament.

230 *gilte*: golden; *sonne*: presumably an aureole.

231 To save him the weight of real gold.

235 *as the gledes rede*: red as glowing coals.

249 *Absolon*: Absalom, son of David, was noted for the luxuriance of his hair.

250 *Ester*: Esther, Jewish maiden during the Captivity, who married the Persian King Ahasuerus, through whom she was able to help her nation.

251 *Jonathas*: Jonathan, the friend of David.

252 *Penalopee*: Penelope, wife of Ulysses; *Marcia Catoun*: Marcia, daughter of Marcus Cato Uticenis, a noble Roman, and noted for the wifely virtues.

254 *Ysoude*: Isolde, in Celtic mythology and heroine of the legend of Tristram; *Eleyne*: Helen of Troy.

255 *al this may disteyne*: outshines all these.

257 *Lavyne*: Lavinia, beloved by Aeneas in the latter part of the *Aeneid*; *Lucresse*: Lucretia, wife of the noble Roman, Tarquinius Collatinus, raped by Sextus Tarquinius, who then killed herself.

258 *Polixene*: Polyxena, daughter of Priam, slain at the sack of Troy.

259 *Cleopatre*: Cleopatra, Queen of Egypt, loved by Julius Caesar and later Mark Antony.

261 *Tisbe*: Thisbe, heroine of the tragic Babylonian story of Pyramus and Thisbe.

263 Hero, Dido and Laodameia were heroines of Greek and Roman legend.

264 *Phillis*: Phyllis hanged herself for love of Demophon and was turned into an almond tree.

265 Canace, daughter of Aeolus, was loved by Macareus.

266 *Ysiphile*: Hypsiphyle, a Lemnian princess, daughter of King Thoas, who figures in the legend of Jason.

267 *boost*: boast.

268 *Ypermnestre*: Hypermnestra, wife of Oicles; *Adriane*: Ariadne, daughter of Minos, King of Crete, who fell in love with Theseus and helped him to escape from the Labyrinth.

The Legend of Cleopatra
lines 580–705

That Cleopatra was not conspicuously 'good' is one reason why it has been suggested that Chaucer was being to some extent ironic in his choice of several of the women in the *Legend*. But, as Robinson points out, it was only necessary that they should be 'good according to the standard of the religion of Love'.

580 *Tholome*: Ptolemy, probably Cleopatra's elder brother, whom she had been intended to marry (as was customary in the Egyptian royal family).

583 *befel there swich a cas*: it so happened.

585 *regnes*: realms, kingdoms.

589 So it happened that, as fortune lured him on to disaster – references abound in medieval literature to the fickleness of fortune.

592 *suster*: Antony was married to Octavia, sister of Caesar Augustus.

593 *or that she was war*: before she realised it.

594 *algates*: at all costs.

595 *tok*: stirred up.

597 *gentil werreyour*: noble warrior.

598 And his death was a great tragedy.

599 *rage*: passion, madness.

600 *las*: snare.

603 *due*: fitting.

605 He thought nothing of dying in battle.

612 *Worthi to*: as worthy as.

615 She became his wife and had him at her command.

616-20 To describe the wedding and the feast would take me too long – for I have undertaken to compose so many stories (i.e. of good women) – and I might skimp the telling of matters of greater relevance and weight. (Surely a typical piece of Chaucerian disingenuity, a politely veiled protest against the task he has been set, in which his interest is clearly not fully engaged.)

622 And so I will at once skip to what matters.

624 *Octovyan*: Antony's brother-in-law, the Emperor Augustus; *wod . . . of*: maddened by.

625 *Shop hym an ost*: got ready a force.

631 *Tok ek his red*: Accordingly took counsel.

633 *stente*: delayed.

635-6 The trumpets sounded, and Antony's men began to cry out and shoot, endeavouring to attack with the sun behind them. (This account of the Battle of Actium is partly based on Plutarch.)

637 *out goth*: is discharged; *gonne*: cannon (an anachronism).

638 And vehemently they all ram each other at once.

640 *grapenel*: grappling hooks; *crokes*: hooks.

641 *sherynge-hokes*: shearing hooks (for cutting ships' ropes).

642-4 'This is wonderfully graphic. A boarder bursts in with a pole-axe; a sailor, on the defence, flees behind the mast, then dashes forward again, and drives the assailant overboard.' (Skeat)

645 He impales him upon his spear's point.

648 *pesen*: an obscurity – editors suggest either hard 'peas' (to make the decks slippery) or 'pitch' (to spread wildfire); *slidere*: slippery.

649 The quicklime was to throw in the enemy's eyes.

652 *schent*: defeated; *put hym*: takes to.

653 *to-go*: scatter.

655 *For strokes*: On account of the blows (aimed at her ships).

659 On this day have I thus lost the one I worship.

661 *rof*: stabbed – Chaucer follows an inaccurate source: Antony killed himself the following year at Alexandria.

662 *or*: ere, before.

668 *of wemen which a trouthe*: how faithful women can be.

672 *shryne*: a tomb for Antony.

676 *let the cors enbaume*: had the corpse embalmed; *fette*: fetched.

677 *shette*: shut.

699 *nadderes*: adders (Chaucer used the original form – about his time the word was changing to the modern form).

702 *storyal*: historical.

703-5 The general sense is: May we not have aching heads up to the time when I find another so true as Antony (as I never shall).

p. 95   The Complaint unto Pity

This poem, if not actually translated from a lost original, owes much to French influence. The title derives from the old French *Complaint*, the technical name for a love poem of a mournful kind addressed to a cruel mistress. The nineteenth-century scholar, Furnivall, considered the *Complaint* to have had autobiographical significance. If not certainly Chaucer's earliest original poem, it is very early and is the first example in English of the seven-line stanza, used later by Chaucer in *Troilus and Criseyde*.

1 *yore agoo*: for such a long time.

4 *with-oute deth*: without actually dying.

11 *awreke*: avenge.

14 Skeat points out the awkwardness of the notion of pity being buried '*in* an herte' and the confusion this causes later in the poem.

16 *swogh*: swoon.

19 *presen*: press on, hasten.

21 *I nas but lorn*: I was all but lost.

26 *cast*: contrived.

27 *redeless of peyne*: without counsel in our suffering.

36 *lustely*: gaily, carelessly.

37 *as thoughte me*: as I thought.

41 *Estaat*: Rank; *Dreed*: Fear.

54 *put . . . up*: withdrawn, pocketed.

58 *coroune*: crown.

59 *rial*: royal. The sense of lines 59–63 may be paraphrased: Your servant (if I dare so call myself) declares to your excellence the fatal distress into which he has fallen, both because of his ill fortune and for the sake of your reputation – as follows.

65 *regalye*: authority.

70 *apertenant*: such as belongs to.

76 *wanten*: are lacking.

77 *lore*: lost.

78 *Maner and Gentilesse*: Courtesy and Good Breeding, Nobility.

82 *but ye the rather take cure*: unless you take care.

86 *fordoo than in a throwe*: destroyed then in an instant.

91 *despeyred*: reduced to despair.

92 *Herenus quene*: Queen of the Furies (Greek, Erynyes). Pity was not herself one of the Furies, but the only person who could control them.

93 *That yow have sought*: Who have sought you.

95 *ever lenger the more*: more and more as time goes on.

97 And though I have no skill in complaint.

105 *bere*: funeral bier.

106 *shewe parcel of*: analyse in detail.

109 *wake or winke*: wake or sleep.

110 *rekke*: care; *flete*: float.

119 *besy*: constant, active.

p. 99 *To Rosemounde*

Addressed to an unidentified woman, this is a ballade, a form much favoured by Chaucer for his shorter poems, and derived from French models. The combination of humour and courtly love is typical of Chaucer, who is clearly indulging in gentle satire on the courtly conventions in love poetry. He manages his three-rhyme pattern with skill and neatness.

2 As far as the map of the world reaches.
8 *daliaunce*: the word connotes any exchange between lovers from gossip to flirtation.
9 *tyne*: large tub.
10 *confounde*: destroy.
11 Your delicate voice that you twist out so finely.
13 So gently I tread in the bonds of love.
17 There was never pike so wallowed in galantine sauce (used for pickling).
20 *Tristam*: Tritsram, pattern of knightly love in Celtic mythology.
21 *refreyde*: 'cool down; lit. "refrigerated".' (Skeat); *affounde*: grow numb with cold.

p. 100   Womanly Noblesse
This title was first given to the poem by Skeat, who considered it to be of doubtful authenticity. Robinson accepts it as certainly by Chaucer.

2 *hoole*: whole, perfect; *governaunce*: demeanour.
7-9 That as long as I live, my heart has chosen you to be its mistress in true and constant resolve never to change, on account of adversity of any kind.
13 *souvenaunce*: remembrance.
14 *duresse*: hardship.
19 *chaunce*: fortune, lot.
20-6 It is difficult to turn this into idiomatic modern English, and perhaps unnecessary. The literal meaning is: awaiting your favour when your nobility is pleased to alleviate my great distress, and with your pity make me prosper somewhat in full abatement of my sadness and thinks it reasonable that womanly magnanimity should not desire to do harm where she finds no lack of submissiveness.
27 *norture*: good breeding.
30 But accept this (poem) out of the goodness of your heart.

p. 101   Chaucers Wordes unto Adam, His Owne Scriveyn
The identity of this scrivener, or copyist, has not been discovered. Chaucer's half-humorous warning to him reminds us of one of the problems of

writing before the introduction of the printing press. The following is a paraphrase:

> Adam my scrivener, if it should ever happen that you have to make further copies of my translation of Boethius or of my *Troilus*, may you have an attack of the scab under your long hair if you don't copy what I wrote more accurately. How often have I had to do your work over again, rubbing and scraping away to correct it, and all because of your carelessness and haste.

p. 102   *The Former Age*

This is freely adapted from Boethius, *De Consolatione Philosophiae*, with the exception of stanzas 5 to 8, which are almost entirely original.

1 *paisible*: peaceful.

3 *helde hem payed of*: were content with.

4 *by usage*: without cultivation.

5 They were not inordinately pampered.

6 *quern*: handmill; *melle*: mill.

7 *pounage*: pig food.

11 'Which they rubbed in their hands, and ate of sparingly.' (Skeat)

12 *forwes*: furrows.

14 *Unkorven and ungrobbed*: unpruned and not dug round.

16 For clarre (a drink made of wine, honey and spices) nor for galantine sauce.

17 *Mader, welde, or wood*: madder, weld or woad (three vegetable dyes); *litestere*: dyer.

19 *egge*: sword.

20 'No one had yet learnt how to distinguish false coins from true ones.' (Skeat) But surely the meaning is that there were no coins known, either false or true.

21 *karf*: carved, ploughed.

22 *fette*: imported; *outlandish*: foreign.

25 *werreye*: make war.

32 *coveytyse*: covetousness, greed.

33-7 'These tyrants [i.e. covetous men] did not gladly venture into battle to win a wilderness or a few bushes where poverty (alone) dwells – as Diogenes says – or where victuals are so scarce and poor that only mast or apples are found there.' (Skeat)

38 *bagges*: moneybags.

39-40 That's where they like to go, stopping at nothing to attack the city with all their forces.

46 *kid*: known; *seurtee*: security.

47 Their hearts were in harmony, with no bitterness.

49 *hauberk*: coat of mail; *plate*: plate armour.

51 Took no delight in quarrelling.

52 *cheryce*: cherish, care for.

54 No overlord, no taxation under tyranny.

56 Skeat suggests as a possibility for this line, missing in the mss.: 'Fulfilled erthe of olde curtesye.' He paraphrases lines 55-6 as follows: 'Humility and peace, (and) good faith (who is) the empress (of all), filled the earth full of ancient courtesy.'

56 *likerous*: lecherous.

57 *delicacye*: wantonness.

58 *Nembrot*: Nimrod, the ambitious king, was thought in the Middle Ages to have built the Tower of Babel.

62 *Doublenesse*: double-dealing, duplicity.

63 *mordre in sondry wyse*: murder in various forms.

p. 104   Fortune

This poem is in the form of three ballades and an envoy. The metrical problem which Chaucer set himself by his choice of a rhyme scheme was considerable, so the poem is something of a technical *tour de force*. The principal source is Boethius, and echoes from the *Roman de la Rose* and perhaps Dante have been traced. The subtitle, referring to an unpainted face, implies a contrast between the straightforwardness of the Pleintif (the pleader against Fortune) and the deceitful face of Fortune.

1 *transmutacioun*: changes of fortune.

2 Now happiness, now misery, now poverty, now honour.

5-7 Nevertheless, the lack of fortune's favour will never make me sing, even to save my life, 'I have wasted all my time and all my effort.'

9-12 The precise meaning is not obvious, but the general drift is: 'Enough of the light of intelligence is left me to know friend from foe when seen in the mirror of Fortune. This much has Fortune's wheel, whirling up and down, taught me to know in a single hour.'

13-14 'But truly, Fortune's violence has no power over him who is master of himself.'

15 *suffisaunce*: self-sufficiency.

7 *Socrates*: Chaucer represents the fifth-century B.C. Greek philosopher a
he champion of moral virtue.

0 *chere*: demeanour, appearance; *savour*: attraction.

1 *colour*: pretence.

2 Her greatest claim to esteem is that she lies.

3 *dissimulour*: deceiver.

5 *but himself it wene*: unless he imagines he is.

7 *kene*: cruel.

9-30 Say thus: 'Enough of all thy plenty which thou hast afforded formerly.'

1 How do you know what future I have in store for you?

2 *thy beste frend*: Skeat considers that this may refer to either John of Gaunt
died 1399) or the King himself.

4 A true friend and one who appears to be a friend.

5-6 Thou hast no need of the gall of a hyena, which cures eyes blinded as a
enance. (This refers to a belief among ancient naturalists.)

7-8 Your anchor still holds, and you may yet arrive at the place where my
avours are distributed with bounty.

3-4 Will you then bind me, your queen, by law to be always at your
ommand?

5 *variaunce*: change, mutability.

7 My teaching is better than your suffering is bad.

9 *dampne*: condemn.

0-1 You cannot take from me my true friends, blind goddess; I thank you
or showing me who my false friends are (i.e. the friends I owe only to my
ood fortune).

2 Take them back; let them all stay together in one crowd.

3-5 'Their niggardliness, in keeping their riches to themselves, foreshews
hat thou wilt attack their stronghold; just as an unnatural appetite precedes
lness.' (Skeat)

7 *pinchest at*: find fault with.

0 *my realtee oppresse*: violate my sovereignty.

2 *welkne*: sky.

3 *kythen my brotelnesse*: display my fickleness.

5-7 What you call fortune is really the execution of the will of God who
rdains all things out of his great wisdom.

9 *sikernesse*: stability.

1 *intresse*: interest, concern.

5-9 'And I (Fortune) will requite you for your trouble (undertaken) at my
equest, whether there be three of you, or two of you (that heed my words).
And, unless it pleases you to relieve him of his pain (yourselves), pray his
est friend, for the honour of his nobility, that he may attain to some better
state.' (Skeat)

This ballade of good counsel derives something, but not much, from
Boethius.

1 *prees*: the world; *sothfastnesse*: adherence to truth.
2 *Suffyce unto thy good*: Be content with what you have.
3 For avarice breeds hatred and ambition is unsure.
4 The world is full of envy and prosperity is everywhere cheated (or possibly
'the hope of well-being is everywhere frustrated'. The editors are silent on
this point.)
5 Have a taste for no more than what becomes you.
6 *that other folk canst rede*: who can advise others.
7 And truth shall make you free, there is no doubt.
8 Do not put yourself into a passion to set right all crookedness.
9 *hir*: i.e. Fortune.
10 'Much repose consists in abstinence from fussiness.' (Skeat)
11 Roughly equivalent to, 'Do not strive to kick against the pricks'.
12 *crokke*: earthenware pitcher – the reference is to the fable in Aesop where
the pitcher is broken against a wall and the brass vessel is not.
13 *Daunte*: Subdue; *otheres dede*: the actions of others.
15 Receive with due submission whatever is sent you.
17 *Her*: Here (on earth).
19 *thy contree*: i.e. heaven.
20 *gost*: spirit.
22 *Vache*: literally Cow (a reference back to 'beste' in line 18).
23 *leve*: cease.
24 *Crye him*: Beg for this.
27 *mede*: reward.

This medieval quality cannot be rendered by any single word in modern
English. It comprises many virtues of which the following are some:
gentleness, nobility, kindness, courtesy, good breeding, high birth. Chaucer's
ballade derives partly from Boethius and partly from a passage in the
Roman de la Rose.

1 *stok*: source (i.e. Christ).
3 *trace*: steps; *alle his wittes dresse*: apply his whole mind.
4 *sewe*: pursue.

-6 For rank should be measured by virtue and not the other way round,
feel safe in asserting.

' *Al were he*: Although he should wear.

| *rightwisnesse*: justice.

| *sobre, pitous, and free*: serious, compassionate and generous.

0 *Clene of his gost*: Pure in spirit.

5 *old richesse*: inherited wealth.

8 That (i.e. virtuous nobility) is the exclusive property of no rank.

0 *queme*: serve.

. 109 Lak of Stedfastnesse

This poem was addressed to King Richard II during the last years of his
and Chaucer's lives. The precise occasion is not known. One of the mss.
as the following note, quoted by Skeat: 'This balade made Geffrey
Chauuciers the Laureall Poete of Albion, and sent it to his souerain lorde
ynge Rycharde the secounde, thane being in his Castell of Windesore.'

Somtyme: Once.

as in conclusioun: in effect.

for mede and wilfulnesse: for the sake of gain and of getting one's own way.

0 *unable*: incapable, feeble.

1 *collusioun*: conspiracy

3 *wrecchednesse*: meanness.

5 *resoun is holden fable*: reason (or right) is held to be an illusion.

8 Judgement is blinded by love of money.

4-5 Allow nothing to be done in your kingdom that is harmful to your
osition.

. 111 The Complaint of Venus

The title of this poem, not given to it by Chaucer but by a copyist, is not
ow thought appropriate, but it is not known to whom the poem was
ddressed. It was partly adapted, partly translated from the French of Sir
Otes de Granson. The envoy is Chaucer's own.

while I may dure: as long as I live.

his: this refers to the above-mentioned lover of the unnamed lady who is
Deaking.

I-12 For grace (by which is meant either God's grace or the favour of his own nature and gifts, or simply good fortune) has chosen so far to advance him that he is the perfect treasure of all knighthood.

17 *suffisaunce*: sufficiency of wealth, position, natural gifts.

19 *werk*: deed; *contenaunce*: demeanour.

21 That I am established in true security.

22 *aventure*: fortune.

25-30 Now certainly, love, it is indeed appropriate that people should pay dearly for your great gift, as by lying awake in bed or fasting at meals, weeping instead of laughing, lament in singing.

34 Her inquisitiveness demands that she know all.

35 *resonable*: innocent.

37-9 'So dearly is love purchased in (return for) what he gives; he often gives inordinately, but bestows more sorrow than pleasure.' (Skeat)

42 *encomberous*: burdensome.

46 *nouncerteyn*: uncertainty.

50 *las*: snare.

52 *lete of*: leave off, cease.

53 *No fors thogh*: It is of no avail that.

54 *sen hym*: see him (i.e. the one I love).

57-60 And indeed, love, when I consider any position that a man may hold, then (I realise that) through your liberality you have made me choose the best that ever walked on earth.

61 *lok thou never stente*: see that you never leave off.

62-3 And may jealousy test my heart and see whether any distress will ever make me change my mind.

66 *the*: thee (i.e. my heart).

68 *entente*: wish.

69 Seek no further, in highway or in byway.

70 *pay*: pleasure.

73 *Princesse*: though some editors have thought that an alternative reading, 'Princes', is the correct one, it seems more likely that the 'Princesse' referred to is Isabel of York, daughter of the King of Spain.

73 *in gre*: in good part.

74-5 Addressed to your great benevolence to the best of my small talent.

76 *elde*: old age.

79 *penaunce*: labour, trouble (i.e. to represent in English the intricacy ('curiosite') of the French original by Granson).

82 *make*: write poetry.

The Scogan here addressed is thought to have been Henry Scogan (1361?–1407), who was tutor to Henry IV's four sons. He was an admirer of Chaucer, who probably wrote this poem when Scogan was about 32. Scogan himself wrote a poem after Chaucer's death, in which he refers to him as his 'maistre'.

2 *creat*: created; *dure*: last.

3 *bryghte goddis sevene*: the seven plants, represented as weeping, wailing and undergoing suffering, because the laws of heaven are broken in pieces. This weeping is taken to refer to the great floods of 1393.

7 *Of which errour*: From ignorance of which.

8 By eternal decree it was formerly ordained.

9 *fyfte sercle*: the fifth heavenly sphere reckoned from outside, i.e. that of the planet Venus.

14 *diluge of pestilence*: pestilential flood.

16 *rekelnesse*: rashness.

18 *for*: because.

21 *erst*: before.

22-4 You in your scorn also made Cupid bear witness to that rebellious word of yours (i.e. in renouncing your love). and for this he will no longer be your lord.

26 *ywroken*: avenged.

27 *oure figure*: i.e. stout – see line 31.

29 *unhap*: misfortune.

30-2 Lest on account of your guilt (i.e. in forswearing love) love's vengeance proceed against all stout, grey-haired men (i.e. like you and me), who are men so likely to succeed in love. A typical piece of Chaucerian humorous irony.

33 *mede*: reward.

35 'See, the old gray-haired man is pleased to rime and amuse himself.' (Skeat – who also points out that if the reading 'Renne' for 'rime' is adopted, the meaning would be 'See, the old gray horse is pleased to run about and play,')

36 *m'excuse*: excuse myself.

37-42 The editors are not helpful here. The general meaning seems to be: 'Certainly, with no rhyme do I contemplate waking up my Muse, who is like a sword rusting in the sheath, always in peace. When I was young, I used her like a sword drawn in battle; but everything men write in prose or verse will pass away; let every writer have his turn in his own time.'

43 *the stremes hed*: this refers to the fact that Scogan was living with the court at Windsor, source of royal favour, and higher up the Thames than Greenwich, where Chaucer was living in retirement.

46 *forgete*: forgotten.

47 Much editorial ink has been expended on the reference to Tullius. The simplest of several conjectures is that the Tullius referred to is Cicero, author of the treatise *De Amicitia (On Friendship)*.

48 Put in a word for your friend where it will bear fruit.

49 Farewell, and see that you never again defy love.

p. 116   Lenvoy de Chaucer a Bukton

The identity of Chaucer's friend has not been established, but he was probably either a Yorkshire or a Suffolk country gentleman about to get married. Half-humorous poems against marriage were a medieval convention and were not intended to be taken too seriously.

2 *sothfastnesse*: steadfastness in truth.

4 *As who saith*: As if saying.

5 *highte*: promised.

8 *eft in swich dotage*: again into such an old man's folly. The death of Philippa, Chaucer's wife, is thought to have occurred in 1387, some time before the date of this poem.

10 *Sathanas*: Satan was commonly represented as perpetually gnawing at the chain by which he was bound.

11-12 But I will go so far as to say that, if Satan were out of his torment, he would never of his own free will consent to be bound again.

13 *eft hath levere*: would rather once more.

15 *dissevere*: be separated.

18 The reference is to I Cor. vii, – 'For it is better to marry than to burn.'

19-20 But your flesh will have sorrow so long as you live, and you will be slave to your wife, as wise men say.

23 That it would be better for you to be taken prisoner in Friesland – a contemporary expression connoting a terrible fate.

25-6 I send you this little piece of proverbial or figurative writing and advise you to take it to heart.

27-8 The general sense of these two proverbs is 'Let well alone' and 'If you enjoy security, don't risk losing it'.

29 *Wyf of Bathe*: i.e. the Prologue to the Wife of Bath's Tale (to which Chaucer's frequent references indicate that he was pleased with it).

30 *Of*: Concerning.

p. 117   The Complaint of Chaucer to his Purse

Complaints of penury addressed to a patron were fairly common in the fourteenth century. Editors have cited various French models, which Chaucer may or may not have had in mind. But, to quote Robinson, 'by whatever poem or poems it was suggested, Chaucer's complaint, with its humorous adaptation of the language of a lover's appeal to his mistress, is certainly one of the happiest variations on the well-worn theme'. According to Skeat, the Envoy to the Complaint dates the poem with precision: Parliament accepted Henry IV as King in September 1399. Almost immediately Chaucer received an additional annual grant, but he only lived a year to enjoy it. This was his last poem.

4 For indeed, unless you take on a heavy appearance – Chaucer is punning on the two senses of 'hevy', weighty (as opposed to 'lyght') and sorrowful.
5 *bere*: bier (on which the coffin is taken to the grave).
11 *yelownesse*: the colour of gold.
16 *as*: while (I am).
17 *out of this toune*: 'This seems to mean – "help me to retire from London to some cheaper place".' (Skeat)
19 *shave*: stripped (of money) as is a friar's head (of hair).
22 Henry IV, exiled by Richard II, took advantage of the rebellion against the King and returned to depose him. Albion was the traditional name for Britain and was first ruled, according to the ancient historians, before the coming of the Romans by Brutus, traditionally supposed to be descended from Aeneas the Trojan.
25 And you that may put right all our ills.

p. 118   Against Women Unconstant

This is generally considered to be authentic Chaucer, but the ascription has been questioned. Style and subject-matter are characteristic.

1 *newefangelnesse*: fondness for novelty.
2 *servaunt*: devotee (in love); *grace*: favour.
5–6 You can't remain faithful to one man for as long as six months, so keen always is your desire for something new.
7 Blue was traditionally the colour of constancy in love and green of inconstancy. (Brides are today supposed to wear 'something blue'.)
8 Just as nothing can leave a permanent impression on a mirror.
9 *lightly*: easily, superficially; *pace*: pass, go.

10 *fareth*: behaves; *werkes*: actions.

11 There is no loyalty your heart is capable of holding to.

13 *and that is sene*: as is most evident.

15-17 You could be canonised as a patron saint of fickleness even more appropriately than (those models of infidelity) Delilah, Cressida and Candace, for you are faithful only to faithlessness.

18 *tache*: fault; *arace*: eradicate.

19 If you lose one (lover), you can easily get two more.

20-1 'This allusion to the wearing of light summer garments seems here to imply wantonness or fickleness. . . . It would seem that green was a favourite colour for summer garments.' (Skeat) But in folklore to wear a green gown is a specific euphemism for making love.

p. 119 *Complaynt D'Amours*
The authorship of this typical medieval love-complaint has been questioned, but it is now accepted as Chaucer's.

3 And is least able to find a cure for his distress.

4-5 *deedly compleininge On hir*: bitter denunciation of her.

7 *That*: refers back to 'me' in line 6; *sleeth me for my trewthe*: slays me for my faithfulness.

8 *may yow lyke*: may please you.

10 *syke*: sigh.

12-13 You have cast me on that hateful island from which no man escapes alive. (According to Robinson, the island is Naxos, where Theseus abandoned Ariadne.)

14 This is my reward, sweetheart, for loving you best.

15-21 The truth is, as seems probable to my thinking, that if it were possible to make a true reckoning of the worth of your beauty and goodness, it would be no wonder that you choose to give me pain; since I, the unworthiest man on horse or on foot, dare to aspire to the height of your favour, I am not surprised that you do not grant me it.

24-8 My song may well be 'My life is spent in sorrow'; but this song may yet be confuted: for mercy, pity and true friendship – so I say, despite my deathly looks – all these made me love you.

32 Who without cause inflict this sorrow on me.

33-4 Yes, indeed (I will forgive her); for my folly is not her responsibility, although she is the cause of my death.

37 *reed*: advice.

41 *doon*: make.

43 *verray rote*: the true root and cause

45 *bote*: cure, remedy.

46 *vouched sauf*: deigned.

47 But does she perhaps take pleasure in my distress?

48 It is her custom to take pleasure.

50-6 But indeed, since she is in my judgement the fairest creature, the most blessed and also the best Nature has ever made or shall ever make so long as the world shall last, what I wonder is, why she so neglects pity: this was indeed a great omission on the part of Nature.

57 Yet all this is no fault of hers, I declare.

60 *othere men*: to other men.

63 And I am content with whatever pleases her.

64-70 Yet I dare, with sorrowful heart, beseech you, of your womanly humility, to let me express in words the pain of my bitter anguish, and to read my complaint once through, for I am sore afraid that, because of my lack of skill, I have here said something to your displeasure.

71 *loth*: hateful.

72 I would be, so help me God.

74 *to*: until.

78-9 I have always been, and ever shall be your true and humble servant, however things go with me, in life or in death.

81 Source of light to the bright, clear star (i.e. Venus, sacred to love).

82 *in oon*: with constancy.

86 *foughel*: bird.

87 *hool*: wholly, entirely.

89 *That*: refers back to 'hir' in line 87.

91 *do me sterve*: kills me.

p. 122 *Merciles Beaute*

Strenuous editorial attempts to find a foreign original for this poem have unearthed no more than a handful of brief and mainly general similarities in French poetry. It cannot be disputed that the whole three-part roundel is thoroughly and richly Chaucerian, especially in its transition from passionate romanticism to cool and resolute irony.

1 *sodenly*: instantly.

2 *sustene*: bear.

3 *kene*: sharply.

4 *but*: unless.

5 *grene*: fresh.

10 *trouthe*: i.e. of my love.

16 For your mercy is held in check by disdain.

17 Thus you have brought about my death, though I am guiltless.

21 *compassed*: enclosed.

23 *sterve for*: dies of.

28 I intend never again to starve in his prison.

31 I do not care, I say just what I think.

34 *ystrike out of his sclat*: struck from his roll.

36 *mene*: way.

p. 124 *Proverbs*

These proverbs are ascribed to Chaucer in two of the mss., but are not certainly his.

1 What is the purpose of all these clothes.

4 *pilche*: furred cloak.

5-8 My arms cannot contain the whole compass of the world; whoever tries to grasp too much will keep hold of little.

GLOSSARY

affrayed: aroused
ago: gone
algate(s): always, in any case, all the same.
attempre: mild, moderate
axen: ask
ay: yes, for ever, always
aye(y)n: again
aye(y)ns: against, before

beforn, *biforn*: before
bespreynt: sprinkled
besy, bisy: busy, active, attentive
bet: better
benigne: kindly
brennen: burn
briddes, bryddes: birds
but if: unless

cas: case
certes, certis: indeed, certainly
chese: choose, chose
cleped: called, named
clerk(e): scholar
corage: heart, spirit, disposition

delytous: delightful
despitous, dispitous: spiteful, cruel, grievous
drede: fear, doubt, awe
dresse: direct

eke, *eek, ek*: also, indeed

elles: else
endyte: write, compose
espy, espie: spy, view, look
everich: every(one), each

fer: far
fo(o): foe
for: because (when not simply *for*)
fro: from

gan, *gonne(n)*: began, or did (as in auxiliary to form past tense)
gilte: golden

han: have
hem: them
hight: is called
hir(e), her: her, their
hit, hyt: it

iolif: jolly

kinde, *kynde*: nature

lasse: less
leef, lief: dear, precious, pleasant
leste(n), liste(n): it pleases, pleased
lite, lyte: little
lorn: lost
lust: desire, pleasure
lusty: gay, carefree, vigorous, pleasant, joyous

maner: kind of
maystow: may you
metten, meten: to dream
mochel: much, great
moo: more
morwe: morning
mowe: may, can

nas: was not
nathele(e)s: nevertheless
ne: not, nor

nis: is not
noght: nothing

obeisaunce: obedience
oo, oon: one

pleynen: to complain, weep

quod: quoth, said

renne: run, ran

sen: see
sentence: meaning, significance, opinion
sey, seye, say: saw (when not simply *say*)
shene: shining, beautiful
shoop: shaped, prepared
siker(ly): sure(ly)
sith(en): since
slee: slay
smal(e): slender, small
solempne: festive, grand
somdel, sumdel: somewhat, something
sonne: sun
so(o)th: truth
sooth to seyn(e): to tell the truth
sorwe: sorrow
soot(e), sote: sweet
steven: voice, sound
stonde: stand
suffre: allow
sweven, swevening: dream
swich: such
swote: sweet
syn: since
sythe: time

than(ne): then (when not simply *than*)
the: thee (when not simply the definite article)
then: than (when not *then*)
ther: where (when not simply *there*)
thilke: this, that, those, these

tho: then
trewely: truly
trow(e): believe, think

un(n)ethe: scarcely, with difficulty

war(e): aware, informed, prudent, discreet, cautious
wedres: weather
welken: heavens, sky
wenen: think, believe
werre: war
wiste: knows, knew
wode, wood: mad
wol: will
wo(o)t: know, knew
wyght, wight: wight, man

y-: prefix indicating a past participle
yaf: gave
ye: yea, yes
ye(n): eye(s)
yive, yeve, yif: give
y-nogh, inowe, enow, enough: enough, in plenty
yow: you
y-wis, ywys: indeed (literally *I know*) – a formal expletive of little significance